THE UK CHURCH IN ACTION

PERCEPTIONS OF SOCIAL JUSTICE AND MISSION IN A CHANGING WORLD

RESEARCH COMMISSIONED BY
WORLD VISION UK, MILTON KEYNES

RESEARCH CONDUCTED BY
BARNA GLOBAL, LONDON

Funding for this research was made possible by the generous support of World Vision UK. Barna Group programmed the surveys and was solely responsible for analysis and writing of the report. Third-party vendors assisted in conducting and hosting surveys for the UK.

Printed in the UK by Bell and Bain Ltd, Glasgow

TABLE OF CONTENTS

T here is much for us to shout about in terms of the difference the Church is making both here in the UK and abroad. I hope you'll find *The UK Church in Action* incredibly helpful in this regard, as it highlights some of the amazing things that churches report actually doing. We may need to turn the volume up though, as this study also reveals that many outside of the Church remain relatively unaware of such an impact, either in their community or the world. In fact, perceptions about and even within the Church vary significantly. The insights from these pages will, I trust, serve as a valuable reference point for you, wherever you are engaged in mission.

At World Vision, our distinctive calling is to bring hope to vulnerable children as a sign of God's unconditional love. They are living in some of the most difficult places in the world, experiencing poverty, conflict, violence and exploitation. We believe every child matters. We also believe we're called, as part of the Church, to be God's agents for change in this world. To achieve this, we partner with people of all faiths or no faith, providing help to all, regardless of faith. Right now, in thousands of communities, our local staff live and work alongside children and families to help change the world they live in for good.

Communities up and down the UK are full of Christ's followers who also have a heart for those living in abject poverty and other heartbreaking circumstances at home and around the world. Church leaders are actively finding ways to meet the needs they see in their communities. The fact is that UK Christians are feeding the hungry, housing the homeless and providing much-needed companionship and friendship to the lonely. They are making a difference, locally and globally. Many see this mission as an integral part of Christian witness and discipleship.

We're called, as part of the Church, to be God's agents for change in this world

But are their communities taking any notice? How are local churches and the UK Church as a whole perceived by non-churchgoers? How are these opinions influenced by the shifting make-up of religious belief in our society?

You will find some of the answers to these questions in the pages that follow. We commissioned this research to create a resource that will equip the Church to be more effective, transforming lives for the sake of the gospel. We are especially thankful for the ministry of Barna Global, whose work enables the Church to reflect on itself, as well as the context in which we find ourselves.

We're also grateful to the key Christian leaders from across a range of denominations and church movements who have contributed to this report, and to those who have helped to shape the qualitative and quantitative research, ensuring it addresses the most pertinent and relevant questions and challenges the Church is facing today.

This report will help you as church leaders to understand how mission and the Church's role in social justice, advocacy and charity are defined today. You'll also learn how effective we're perceived to be in these areas, according to those who lead, attend or do not attend church.

Our prayer is that you will be inspired and challenged by what you read, that the findings will prove useful to you in your ministry and that, together, we might be better able to shine God's light in the darkest places of our communities, turning people toward him. We stand with you and would love to join further with you in that mission, journeying onward together.

TIM PILKINGTON

Chief Executive of World Vision UK

Pilkington is chief executive of World Vision UK, overseeing strategy, direction and performance toward the organisation's mission 'to inspire the UK to take action that transforms the lives of the world's poorest children'. Pilkington joined World Vision UK in 2013 as director of finance & risk and as company secretary, bringing together his skills, his Christian faith and his passion for making a difference in the lives of children. He lives near Cambridge with his wife, Gail, and two teenage children. He's an active member of his local church and serves on the committee of his local youth initiative.

AT A GLANCE

MANY IN THE UK ARE UNAWARE OF THE GOOD WORK OF THE CHURCH

Non-Christians are just as likely to not know about the UK Church's impact in the world (40%) as they are to have a negative opinion of it (41%).

... OR OFFER MIXED REVIEWS.

Though one in four (26%) still calls the Church 'good for the community', most of the general public's assumptions about the Church are unflattering.

ABOUT ONE-THIRD OF UK ADULTS (31%) STRUGGLES TO IDENTIFY NEEDS THE CHURCH SHOULD MEET.

Services for the elderly and the homeless are areas in which the public is most open to the Church's involvement.

ACTIVE CHRISTIANS COULD HELP ADDRESS THE CHURCH'S IMAGE PROBLEM.

This group is highly engaged with and optimistic about the Church and envisions it playing a broad role in the community.

WHAT GOOD IS THE CHURCH?

How do UK adults feel about the Church?

For the most part ... well, they are unsure.

A significant proportion of UK adults (36%), particularly non-Christians (40%), says they don't know whether the Church makes a positive difference in the world. They are even less aware of the effects of local churches in their communities (39% of all adults, 44% of non-Christians)—in fact, one-third (31%) can't even think of a regional need that should fall under the purview of Christian churches. Though they primarily give the Church a positive assessment, even many Christians in the UK report being uncertain of the global (31%) or local (32%) significance of their religious institution.

It seems that the Church in the UK doesn't make a strong impression. Further, those who do draw conclusions about the Church's influence

> A significant proportion of UK adults, particularly non-Christians, says they don't know whether the Church makes a positive difference in the world

offer mixed reviews. About one in three UK adults sees the Church as a benefit to the world (33%) or their own community (35%), though not much more than the proportion who *disagrees* it has a positive impact (31% globally, 26% locally). Those outside the Christian faith are unsurprisingly the most sceptical of its potential, globally (41%) and locally (35%).

'CHRISTIAN CHURCHES IN THE UK ARE MAKING A POSITIVE DIFFERENCE IN THE WORLD'

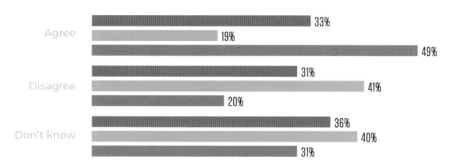

- All British adults
- Non-Christians
- Christians

Agree
- 33%
- 19%
- 49%

Disagree
- 31%
- 41%
- 20%

Don't know
- 36%
- 40%
- 31%

'LOCAL CHRISTIAN CHURCHES ARE MAKING A POSITIVE DIFFERENCE IN MY COMMUNITY'

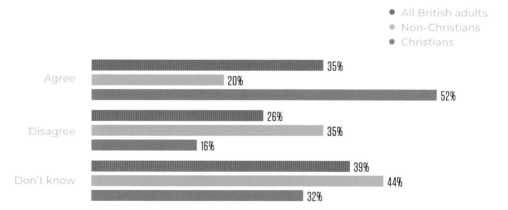

- All British adults
- Non-Christians
- Christians

Agree
- 35%
- 20%
- 52%

Disagree
- 26%
- 35%
- 16%

Don't know
- 39%
- 44%
- 32%

April 2017, n=2,054 British adults

If you're a church leader in the UK who is surprised to read of these unfavourable opinions of the Church, you're not alone: This Barna study shows that nearly half of church leaders assume that non-Christians still celebrate the UK Church's global impact (47% 'strongly' + 'somewhat' agree). The gap in perceptions grows wider when focusing locally; a large majority of church leaders (86% 'strongly' + 'somewhat') agrees non-Christians welcome churches' community presence—but, in reality, just one in five non-Christian adults (20%) says they do.

Where does this dissonance originate? Why are so many people oblivious to the ways in which the UK Church blesses individuals, neighbourhoods and nations? And why are so many church leaders oblivious to the indifferent, and at times adverse, attitudes toward their ministries?

To clarify—and hopefully improve—the Church's reputation in the UK, it's helpful to first understand how the public presently describes it.

FINDING ADJECTIVES FOR CHURCH

UK adults see a mixture of good and bad characteristics in the Christian Church—but some of the most common ones they select from a list of potential options aren't too flattering. Unfortunately, it seems Christian communities strike the general public as hypocritical (24%), judgmental (23%) or anti-science (20%). On the other hand, they are rarely noted for being relevant (9%), being generous (7%) or assisting people with economic needs (5%), even though about a quarter of people (26%) still calls the Church 'good for the community'. Continuing the trend of disconnection from the Church, three in 10 select none of the adjectives or 'don't know', implying they either have no opinion or another one in mind—positive or negative—about the Church.

Non-Christians (a category that includes those of other faiths too) feel strongly pessimistic about the Church (34% 'judgmental', 33% 'hypocritical', 30% 'not compatible with science')—which isn't a big surprise, considering just one percent of non-Christians see the institution as personally applicable to their lives and, as the following chart details, they don't associate the Church with being particularly hopeful or helpful. UK adults who claim no faith at all are even less likely than those of other faiths to see the bright sides of Christianity.

A WINDOW INTO THE UK CHURCH

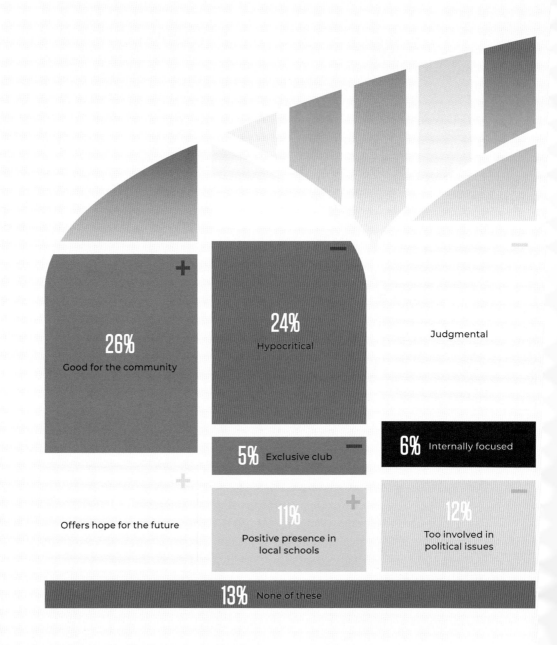

26% Good for the community

24% Hypocritical

Judgmental

5% Exclusive club

6% Internally focused

Offers hope for the future

11% Positive presence in local schools

12% Too involved in political issues

13% None of these

How does the general public describe the Christian Church? Though more than a quarter still feels it's good for their community, some of the most common opinions are negative ones. Three in 10 British adults don't know or don't choose any adjectives for the Church.

+ Positive perceptions
— Negative perceptions

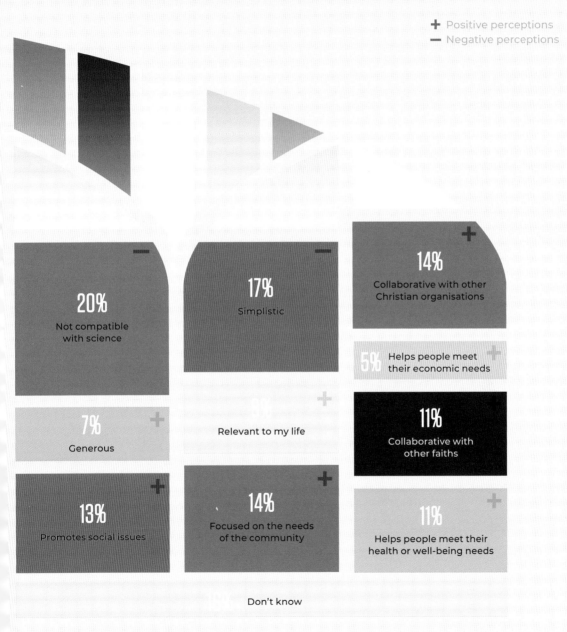

—

20%
Not compatible with science

—

17%
Simplistic

+

14%
Collaborative with other Christian organisations

+

5% Helps people meet their economic needs

+

7%
Generous

+

Relevant to my life

11%
Collaborative with other faiths

+

13%
Promotes social issues

+

14%
Focused on the needs of the community

+

11%
Helps people meet their health or well-being needs

Don't know

April 2017, n=2,054 British adults.

Some of this antagonism toward the Church in general might be tempered, however, or at least set aside within the context of *personal* relationships with people of faith. For instance, a 2015 Barna study showed that the two-thirds of non-Christians in the UK (67%) who reported knowing a Christian were quick to associate these peers with positive traits like being friendly (64%) or caring (52%). Even the most commonly chosen negative quality—narrow-mindedness—was only applied by 13 percent of non-Christians who had a connection with a Christian.[1] Non-Christians' acceptance of individual Christians might seem at odds with a blanket aversion or indifference toward their Church, but it also speaks to the power of personal, everyday interactions that bridge faith segments.

OPINIONS OF THE CHRISTIAN CHURCH, BY FAITH

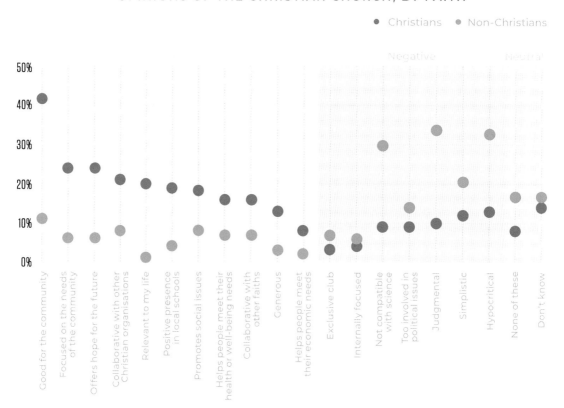

April 2017, *n* = 2,054 British adults.

Christians, meanwhile, have a consistently more promising take on the Church and describe a religious body that is vital, collaborative and dynamic. One in four praises the UK Church for focusing on community needs (24%) and offering hope for the future (24%). Roughly one-fifth believes the Church is a positive presence in schools (19%) and a promoter of social issues (18%). Interestingly, though non-Christians don't perceive this same level of civil engagement (8% say it promotes social issues), they are also more likely to believe Christians are already *too* involved in political issues (14%, compared to 9% of Christians).

An adult's generation seems to be connected to their perceptions of the Church. Different age groups hold a peculiar combination of good and bad assumptions of the Church. For instance, those who are younger than 45 are significantly less likely than adults 45 and older to say the Church is good for the community (18% vs. 32%), even though they are slightly more willing to describe it as generous (10% vs. 6%).

A main reason for some of these generational differences is that Christians are an aging population, with much greater representation among older adults in the UK. For instance, two-thirds of those age 65 and older (67%) self-identify as Christian, compared to about one-quarter of those between ages 18 and 34 (26%). It makes sense then that, with less exposure to the Church or belief in Christianity, the younger the adult, the more likely they are to say they 'don't know' what the Church is like; this is a top response from this younger cohort (21%), another 14 percent of whom select none of the descriptors. In contrast, just 11 percent of adults aged 65 and older say they lack familiarity with the Church. Due to this correlation of youth and non-affiliation, regression analysis reveals that faith, rather than age alone, is a primary factor in many of these generational gaps in perceptions of the Church.

Ethnic minorities in the UK are another demographic segment with a lower rate of Christianity (23%)—though, in their case, this affiliation doesn't seem to hinder a relatively welcoming posture toward the work of the Church. Non-white adults, many of whom adhere to other religions, still regularly deem the Church as good for the community (33%) and attuned to public needs (20%). One in four (24%) believes the Church offers hope for the future, and roughly one in five says it collaborates with other Christian organisations (19%) and helps people with their well-being (18%). Meanwhile,

An adult's age seems to have significant influence on perceptions of the Church

PROPORTION OF EACH AGE GROUP THAT IDENTIFIES AS CHRISTIAN

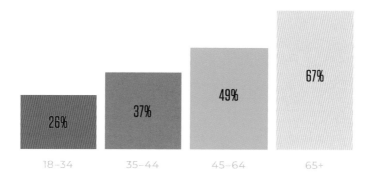

26%	37%	49%	67%
18–34	35–44	45–64	65+

April 2017, n=2,054 British adults.

smaller proportions of ethnic minorities see the faith as judgmental (17%), hypocritical (11%), simplistic (10%) or at odds with science (8%).

WHAT PEOPLE WANT FROM CHURCHES

Despite their vague or poor perceptions of the Church, do UK adults recognise opportunities for the Church to be more involved or to help specific groups?

Active Christians (UK adults who engage in at least monthly church attendance, Bible reading and prayer) see the Church playing a broad role in UK communities and offering a wide spectrum of services, from financial relief to children's ministry. These active Christians, primarily affiliated with the Church of England (43%), stand out from the general population overall in their regular engagement with the local church—nearly all (96%) report attending a service about weekly or more often—as well as their higher expectations of the UK Church as a whole.

In contrast, two in five UK adults (41%) either don't see a local role for the Church or can't imagine what it would be. Fittingly, the respondents who do not report that the Church makes a positive difference in their community also identify fewer opportunities for the Church to do so. This suggests that they don't see value in the Church because of presuppositions about its nature or capability, rather than its level of effort.

JUST HOW ENGAGED ARE ACTIVE CHRISTIANS?

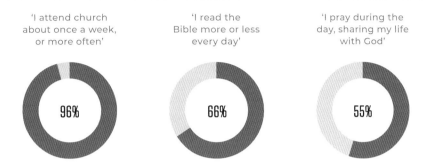

'I attend church about once a week, or more often'

96%

'I read the Bible more or less every day'

66%

'I pray during the day, sharing my life with God'

55%

April 2017, *n*=1,170 active UK Christians.

The UK adults who find some value in the Church's leadership prefer that it be concentrated on the homeless and elderly. About three in 10 want the Church to provide events for the elderly (30%), or night shelters, food and clothes for those without a home (28%). Other services they think churches could help with include collecting meals, toys and clothes for donations (23%), youth clubs and events (23%) and community events such as groups for parents and toddlers or church cafés (20%). Non-Christians follow close behind the general public in most of these expectations, though, as mentioned earlier, they are especially likely to not know of or not offer a suggestion for the Church's local involvement.

> The UK adults who see value in the Church's leadership prefer that it be concentrated on the homeless and elderly

MOST UK ADULTS SEE SOME ROLE FOR THE CHURCH

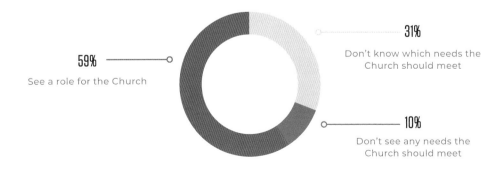

59%
See a role for the Church

31%
Don't know which needs the Church should meet

10%
Don't see any needs the Church should meet

WHAT DO UK ADULTS FEEL CHRISTIAN CHURCHES COULD PROVIDE FOR THE COMMUNITY?

● All British adults   ● Non-Christians   ● Active Christians

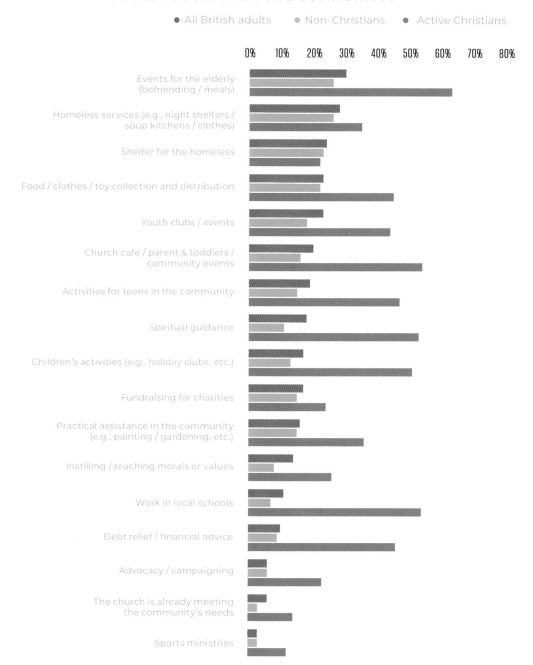

April 2017, n=2,054 British adults; n=1,170 active UK Christians

The pattern among active Christians is much more zealous when discussing any of the above options (63% choose elderly events, 35% choose homeless services, 45% choose collection and donation of goods, 54% choose community and family events), as well as work in local schools (54%), spiritual guidance (53%) and children's activities such as holiday clubs (51%).

When asked to identify what they think the top priorities of their church should be, active Christians emphasise experiences associated with church attendance, like worship (55%) and discipleship (58%). It's noteworthy that engaged Christians see the principal role of the Church as being spiritual and personal, rather than outward-focused. But that doesn't mean they don't want their church to look beyond its own walls. In fact, active Christians are even more likely than their leaders to prioritise serving those in need (47% and 35%, respectively)– which is close to the *lowest* priority for church leaders, producing the largest gap among congregants' and leaders' reported goals. Meanwhile, church leaders are more concerned with one of their central

GENERAL MINISTRY PRIORITIES

Which of the following do you think should be top priorities at your church?

Church leaders
● Active Christians

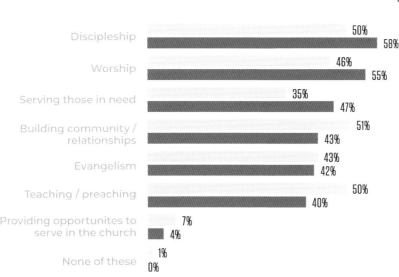

Discipleship — 50% / 58%
Worship — 46% / 55%
Serving those in need — 35% / 47%
Building community / relationships — 51% / 43%
Evangelism — 43% / 42%
Teaching / preaching — 50% / 40%
Providing opportunites to serve in the church — 7% / 4%
None of these — 1% / 0%

April 2017, n=1,170 active UK Christians; April–May 2017, n=302 UK church leaders.

weekly tasks; half believe teaching and preaching should be a top priority (50%, compared to 40% of active Christians).

Age also seems to impact these overall priorities. For example, older Christians are more likely to choose worship (62%), which is important to only a minority of Christians younger than 45 (39%). These generational divides in both community and ministry priorities set the stage for tensions in churches with age diversity—or may reveal blind spots for churches who have a more generationally homogenous congregation.

Overall, UK church leaders are often liable to overestimate the public's goodwill toward the Church, and the UK public is liable to underestimate how much good the Church can do. What is being lost in translation?

In the next chapter, we'll decipher some of the common terms and theories related to the Church's transformative work in the UK and around the world.

Church leaders are often liable to overestimate the public's goodwill toward the Church, and the public is liable to underestimate how much good the Church can do

WHY WE DO WHAT WE DO

Q How can we help the UK Church stand with some of the world's most vulnerable communities (the homeless, elderly, children, refugees, etc.) and demonstrate together the difference that faith is making?

I'm not sure that this is quite the right question: Up and down the country, churches and members of churches are working hard in food banks, night shelters, lunch clubs, before and after school care, toddlers and pre-school clubs as well as caring for refugees in a variety of ways. In my view, what we need to do is to get better at talking about why Christian faith motivates us to show the love of Christ in the world—the 'why we do what we do' question. It is this that will help those outside the Church to understand us better and will remind Christians that this kind of action is an integral and fundamental part of our life in Christ.

Q How can churches develop meaningful, innovative connections with relevant social justice agendas?

Part of the key to this is developing a proper understanding of Christian faith. So often today, society insists that faith is private, internal

DR. PAULA GOODER

Writer and lecturer

Dr. Gooder is a writer and lecturer in biblical studies. Her research areas focus on the writings of Paul the Apostle, with a particular focus on 2 Corinthians and on Paul's understanding of the Church Body. Her passion is to ignite people's enthusiasm for reading the Bible today by presenting the best of biblical scholarship in an accessible and interesting way. Gooder works full-time for the Church of England as the director of mission learning and development in the Birmingham Diocese.

and / or spiritual—in other words, that it has nothing to do with everyday life. This is something we need to resist whenever we can. It is no good to say that we believe that God created the world if we don't then demonstrate our passionate commitment to care for it through our words and actions. Equally, it makes no sense to say that we believe that Jesus loves the lost, the broken-hearted and those on the margins of society if we then do nothing about that ourselves. Following Jesus is a whole-life adventure, not just something we do with our minds. Once we recognise this, we can do nothing other than live this out through making meaningful, innovative connections with a whole range of social justice agendas.

> 'It makes no sense to say that we believe that Jesus loves the lost, the broken-hearted and those on the margins of society if we then do nothing about that ourselves'

Q How can church leaders in the UK learn from global faith and community development to help churches in the UK effect change more successfully?

One of the challenges of the many pressures that Christian leaders experience in the 21st century is that they are often so busy that it can be hard to find the time to stop and drink in the wisdom of others. As with many issues, however, part of the issue is intentionality—the simple recognition that others working in areas like global faith and community development have a wisdom that will inform and transform what we are doing and encourage us to look outwards to learn from what others are doing. More specifically, seeking out the stories of transformation—as well as the actions that brought that transformation about—is one of the best ways to begin that learning.

Q What are some practical ways that UK church leaders might address the Church's 'PR problem'? How can they better embrace or communicate the mission of their faith publicly?

It can be enormously dispiriting to hear how Christians are perceived by non-Christians. So often we are experienced as people who like to say 'no' and who love rules and regulations. At the same time, there are many Christians engaged in a wide variety of activities within their communities who are either unaware or unable to articulate that what they are doing relates to their faith in Jesus Christ. We need to become much more confident in declaring simply and clearly why we do what we do. In many ways this is connected to the command in 1 Peter 3:15: 'Always be prepared to give an answer to everyone who asks you to give the reason for the hope that you have' (NIV). If every Christian knew why they do what they do and said so regularly 'with gentleness and respect', we would be in a very different place than we are now.

AT A GLANCE

UK CHURCH LEADERS PRIMARILY ASSOCIATE 'SOCIAL JUSTICE' WITH ADVOCACY OR WORKING FOR THE COMMON GOOD OF OTHERS.

Meanwhile, 'mission' is commonly defined as proclaiming the truth of Jesus Christ.

THE CHURCH REGARDS SOCIAL JUSTICE AS A CRUCIAL COMPONENT IN THE CHURCH'S MISSION.

Active Christians and church leaders agree that there should be equal emphasis on evangelism and justice work.

MOST CHURCH LEADERS MEASURE THE SUCCESS OF MISSION INFORMALLY, BY OBSERVING THE CHANGES IN PEOPLE'S LIVES.

Younger leaders, however, are more preoccupied with numbers—of commitments to Christ, of weekly attendees and so on.

ACTIVE CHRISTIANS ARE MOSTLY PLEASED WITH HOW THEIR OWN CHURCH IS REACHING OTHERS.

A majority rates it as at least fairly effective, though they see room for improvement on a global level.

SOCIAL JUSTICE AND MISSION

2

When UK adults, and non-Christians in particular, hesitate to offer firm conclusions about the Church's impact or offerings, it indicates that some have a lack of positive ideas about Christianity. Yet in these vague responses there is also an invitation for the Church to better present—and represent—its work to UK society.

'Social justice' and 'mission' are central ideas in the conversation (or, at times, the debate) about the Church's contributions. Even four decades since the First International Congress on World Evangelization in 1974, when evangelists Billy Graham and John Stott led a committee to ultimately 'affirm that evangelism and socio-political involvement are both part of our Christian duty', the Church continues to grapple with how to balance these objectives—or how to define these terms in the first place.[2]

A PROFILE OF UK CHURCH LEADERS IN THIS STUDY

POSITION:

Barna's sample of church leaders is mostly made up of those with a full-time, paid ministry position (83%), rather than other part-time and / or volunteer roles.

LOCATION:

Forty-two percent of church leaders say their congregation is in a town. Three in 10 (30%) minister in an urban setting. Smaller percentages are located in rural (16%) or small cities (11%).

DENOMINATION:

Leaders are distributed across a wide range of denominational affiliations. The most common is Anglican / Church of England (30%)—especially in non-urban settings (37%)—followed by Baptist (14%) and Roman Catholic (10%).

AGE:

As with practising Christians in general, church leaders are an aging group; more than three-quarters of those surveyed (79%) are 45 and older.

Barna gave church leaders in the UK a list of possible definitions for the key concepts of 'social justice' and 'mission' and asked them to select the most fitting ones. They usually associate 'social justice' with advocacy 'on behalf of those who are less fortunate' (27%) or 'everyone working for the common good of all' (24%). 'Mission' is primarily defined by these church leaders evangelistically, as 'actively and intentionally proclaiming the truth of Jesus Christ wherever you are' (42%), though more than a quarter (27%) views it as 'bringing transformation in the world to make it more like the Kingdom of God'. It's interesting that the possible definition for 'mission' which includes justice language ('an all-encompassing word for social justice, advocacy and relief work') wasn't selected by *any* of the church leaders surveyed, indicating that many church leaders see the two movements as distinct, even if complementary. Indeed, when asked to describe the relationship between mission and justice, three-quarters of church leaders (76%) say they are 'different, but integral to each other'.

UK CHURCH LEADERS' DEFINITIONS OF 'SOCIAL JUSTICE'

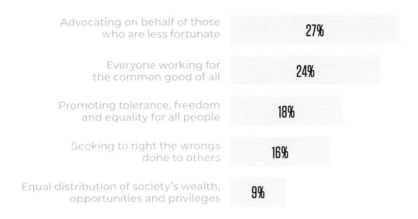

Advocating on behalf of those who are less fortunate — 27%

Everyone working for the common good of all — 24%

Promoting tolerance, freedom and equality for all people — 18%

Seeking to right the wrongs done to others — 16%

Equal distribution of society's wealth, opportunities and privileges — 9%

UK CHURCH LEADERS' DEFINITIONS OF 'MISSION'

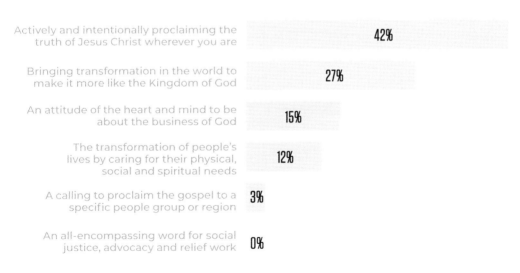

Actively and intentionally proclaiming the truth of Jesus Christ wherever you are — 42%

Bringing transformation in the world to make it more like the Kingdom of God — 27%

An attitude of the heart and mind to be about the business of God — 15%

The transformation of people's lives by caring for their physical, social and spiritual needs — 12%

A calling to proclaim the gospel to a specific people group or region — 3%

An all-encompassing word for social justice, advocacy and relief work — 0%

April - May 2017, n=302 UK church leaders.

BALANCING WORDS AND WORKS

When surveying active Christians, Barna presented set, holistic definitions of 'social justice' ('addressing the physical, social and spiritual needs of another and advocating on their behalf') and 'mission' ('proclaiming the gospel and demonstrating the transformational love of Christ by caring for others and addressing their physical, social and spiritual needs').

With these somewhat comparable ideas in mind, active Christians in the UK are most likely to say that social justice and evangelism have equal importance today (45%). Thirty-eight percent of active Christians, however, say mission today is less focused on evangelism and now places more emphasis on social justice. Only about one in 10 (11%) sees the opposite effect: that the Church is increasingly focused on evangelism, rather than on social justice. Overall, their responses are in line with UK church leaders', who tend to feel social justice has either emerged as a priority (39%) or is on par with evangelism (39%).

> Active Christians in the UK are most likely to say that social justice and evangelism have equal importance today

ACTIVE CHRISTIANS IN THE UK SAY MISSION …

Evangelism

Social Justice

11%

45%

38%

Is less focused on social justice, more focused on evangelism

Places equal importance on social justice and evangelism

Is less focused on evangelism, more focused on social justice

Don't know=6%
April 2017, n=1,170 active UK Christians.

Regardless of the way they describe the balance between proclaiming the gospel in words or in works, active Christians seem to like what they see (or see what they like). A majority of those who detect an emphasis on evangelism (65%) wants churches to focus on evangelism, while a majority of those who recognise an emphasis on social justice (58%) wants churches to prioritise serving people in need.

HOW THE CHURCH GRADES ITSELF

What does success in local mission look like to UK church leaders? Mainly, they assess it by an intangible yet far-reaching metric: 'the extent of the change or difference made in people's lives' (69%). Some church leaders look for something more quantifiable, like the number of people who heard the gospel or learned about Jesus (42%), the number of people helped (35%) or the number of people who decided to follow Jesus after hearing the gospel (32%). More than a quarter of church leaders (27%) regards weekly worship attendance as an indication of local success in mission, though they are less concerned with the number of *new* people at these services (10%).

CHURCH LEADERS' METRICS OF SUCCESS IN MISSION BY AGE

select up to three

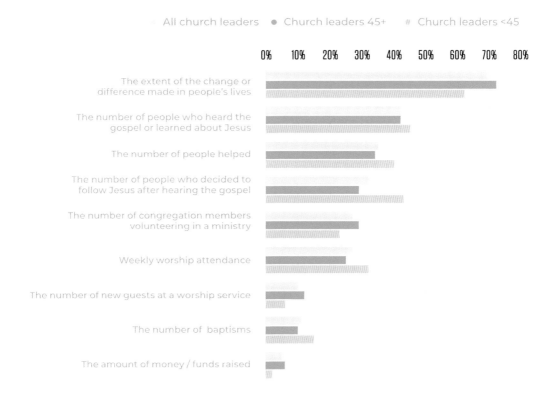

April–May 2017, *n*=186 UK church leaders.

MILESTONES IN THE UK CHURCH'S WORK

The following is a list of measurable objectives or goals a church may have, related to mission.
Which, if any, does your church regularly track? Select all that apply.

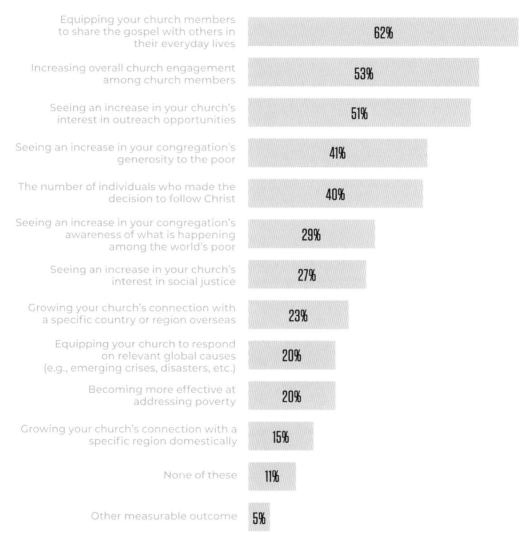

Equipping your church members to share the gospel with others in their everyday lives	62%
Increasing overall church engagement among church members	53%
Seeing an increase in your church's interest in outreach opportunities	51%
Seeing an increase in your congregation's generosity to the poor	41%
The number of individuals who made the decision to follow Christ	40%
Seeing an increase in your congregation's awareness of what is happening among the world's poor	29%
Seeing an increase in your church's interest in social justice	27%
Growing your church's connection with a specific country or region overseas	23%
Equipping your church to respond on relevant global causes (e.g., emerging crises, disasters, etc.)	20%
Becoming more effective at addressing poverty	20%
Growing your church's connection with a specific region domestically	15%
None of these	11%
Other measurable outcome	5%

April–May 2017. *n*=186 UK church leaders.

Younger church leaders are more likely to feel success is reflected in how many people have made a commitment to follow Christ (43% of those under age 45, compared to 29% of church leaders over age 45). It's possible, considering that fewer people in their generations are Christians, conversion carries a profound sense of urgency for this younger group of pastors.

So, what goals do churches actually work toward, given that some of these signs of success are deeply spiritual and perhaps incalculable?

Nearly two-thirds of UK church leaders (62%) see mission's ultimate goal as preparing their own members to be more effective witnesses; their objective is to equip their members to share the gospel with others in their everyday lives. A majority also focuses on tracking increases in overall church engagement among members (53%) or interest in outreach opportunities (51%). All three of these outcomes point to church leaders as being most concerned with the growth and spiritual development of their people, more so than the results of the mission work. In other words: Church leaders see mission first and foremost as a discipleship tool.

They seem less concerned with monitoring congregants' connection to various international or social justice needs, though they do watch for an increased interest in opportunities for outreach or caring for the poor. However,

ACTIVE CHRISTIANS RATE THEIR CHURCHES' EFFECTIVENESS IN MISSION

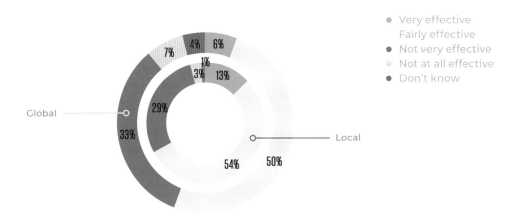

- Very effective
- Fairly effective
- Not very effective
- Not at all effective
- Don't know

April 2017. *n* = 1,170 active UK Christians.

as this particular question was specific to *mission* goals, it's possible these responses simply underscore church leaders' tendency to relegate 'mission' and 'social justice' to somewhat different realms, rather than an actual disinterest in other global, social needs.

However UK Church leaders choose to judge outreach outcomes, its laypeople are mostly encouraged by its involvement. A majority of active Christians sees their church as at least fairly effective in its mission work, whether locally (67%) or globally (56%).

What kind of programmes and endeavours do churches in the UK actually offer? In the next chapter, we'll examine how churches put their priorities into practice.

IN WORDS AND ACTIONS

A Q&A WITH ROY CROWNE

Q How can we help the UK Church stand with some of the world's most vulnerable communities (the homeless, elderly, children, refugees, etc.) and demonstrate together the difference that faith is making?

As Christians, we are called to share the life-changing news of Jesus—both speaking about our faith as well as demonstrating his love through acts of service. Words and actions need to be part of the DNA of every church: in the teaching from the pulpit and in the youth and children's work; through our hospitality as extended families and our integrity in the workplace; in the outward focus of our small groups; and in the way we work together with other churches, local ministries and civic bodies. Our faith becomes authentic when our love for God is expressed in our love for our neighbours, without compromising our obedience to Jesus' call to make disciples. We help churches to stand with the vulnerable when we present an accurate vision of Jesus and teach our congregation to be his courageous, Spirit-filled and sacrificial followers.

ROY CROWNE

Executive Director of HOPE

Crowne was brought up in London's East End. Convinced that no one is beyond hope, he spends his life bringing that good news to people in prisons, villages, towns and cities. Crowne worked for Youth for Christ for 28 years, the last 13 years as national director. He then founded HOPE 08 alongside Mike Pilavachi and Andy Hawthorne to mobilise the Church in mission using words and actions. In 2011, he became HOPE's executive director, seeking to organise the whole Church to work together to make Jesus known in villages, towns and cities throughout the UK.

Q How can churches develop
meaningful, innovative
connections with relevant social
justice agendas?

Jesus modelled mission in words and action. When we follow his example, the Good News is experienced as well as heard. Jesus called us to be united when he prayed to his heavenly Father that his followers would be one so 'the world will know that you sent me and that you love them as much as you love me' (John 17:23, NIV). When we come together, focusing on Jesus and what we have in common, we can have a significant impact in our communities. Together, our voice can be heard as we

> 'Together, our voice can be heard as we speak out for social justice. It can be easier to stay in our own silos or to be side-tracked into debates on doctrine'

speak out for social justice. It can be easier to stay in our own silos or to be side-tracked into debates on doctrine. But we need to be intentional about working together—and often we need to be the one to take the first step, always keeping our focus on Jesus and what he would do in every situation.

Q How do you approach the
balance between both
proclaiming the gospel and living
it out through justice work? How do
you encourage leaders to determine
what that looks like in their own
churches and communities?

Since HOPE began in 2008, we have stressed the importance of words and action as churches work together to make Jesus known. There were churches who were great when it came to preaching the gospel—but they had forgotten that the Bible is always a book in translation, and the most effective translation is our own lives. And there were churches that were fantastic when it came to putting the Christian faith into action, but the people they served didn't know that these churches were serving them in the name of Jesus. Over the past 10 years, we have been thrilled to see churches coming together to serve local communities with foodbanks, winter night shelters, Street Pastors, community chaplains and many more creative expressions of Christian service, which are making Jesus known with words and action together. It is a legacy HOPE has sought to leave as we have worked in partnership with churches across the spectrum of denominations and ethnicities. This sacrificial service looks different in every community as local churches pray and respond to local needs with God's help.

AT A GLANCE

POVERTY ASSISTANCE TOPS THE LIST OF WAYS THE CHURCH HOPES TO PURSUE SOCIAL JUSTICE.
Accordingly, church leaders say their churches are 'very' involved in helping the poor (47%) or vulnerable (32%) in the UK.

ACTIVE CHRISTIANS ARE PERHAPS MORE INTERNATIONALLY FOCUSED THAN THEIR LEADERS.
Their interest in global poverty assistance exceeds church leaders' (53% vs. 40%) and two-thirds (65%) say global and local efforts should be given equal attention.

FOR THE MOST PART, UK CHURCH LEADERS ARE MAKING GOOD ON THEIR EXPRESSED PRIORITIES.
Churches commonly offer pastoral care, host events for the elderly, donate food and other goods or work in local schools.

THE SIZE OF THE CHURCH IS CORRELATED WITH THE AVAILABILITY OF RESOURCES AND ACTIVITIES FOR THE COMMUNITY.
Youth gatherings, homeless services and short-term trips are some of the ministries more prevalent among larger congregations.

THE UK CHURCH: A CURRENT PORTRAIT

3

It's clear that UK adults have some vision of what they'd like to see Christians doing for the world—even though they don't always have the familiarity or confidence to count on the Church for these things. But Barna's survey shows their ideas track pretty closely with the ministry priorities of church leaders, and churches are actually already engaging in these (and many other) movements. This perhaps further illustrates that ambivalence toward the UK Church is not a result of a lack of good work among Christians, but rather a lack of public awareness or recognition of it. Even when the Church's generosity does make headlines—such as the estimated £3 billion worth of hours that religious groups contribute to social projects, like food banks and drop-in centres in the UK—this kind of coverage does not seem to register in UK adults' perceptions of the Church's work.[3]

Consider this chapter one way of helping churches get the word out: In the following pages, Barna's study turns to insiders of the UK Church for an updated account of its aims and activities.

CONNECTING PRIORITIES AND MINISTRIES

UK church leaders were presented with a list of possible functions of a typical ministry and were asked to identify: 1) any activities their church engages in,

UK CHURCHES' ENGAGEMENT OFTEN EXCEEDS THEIR PRIORITIES

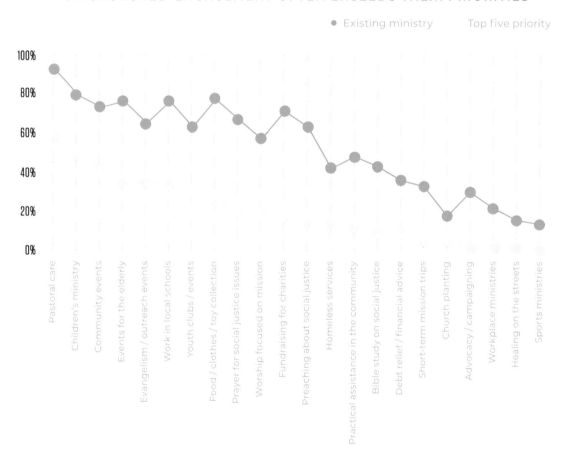

● Existing ministry   Top five priority

April–May 2017. n=302 UK church leaders.

and 2) activities that would fall into their top five mission priorities. There are some inconsistencies between priority and action, but, overall, church leaders tend to offer a picture of ministries that follow through, engaging at least somewhat with their ambitions. Additionally, you'll recall from chapter one that many of these existing projects and ministries address community needs the public hopes churches might meet.

By far the most popular way that UK churches serve people, according to church leaders, is through general pastoral care, which typically includes duties such as visitation or counselling for bereavement (92%). Accordingly, a majority of church leaders—almost six in 10 (58%)—lists this as a top priority for their church. Roughly three-quarters of church leaders say their churches also offer a children's ministry (79%), collect items such as food, toys and clothes for donation (77%), host events for the elderly (76%) and work in local schools (76%).

Larger churches of at least 100 people typically have more willing hands and physical resources than smaller churches for common activities like youth gatherings (78% and 51%, respectively), practical assistance in the community (61% and 37%, respectively) or homeless services (55% and 32%, respectively), as well as rare offerings, like short-term trips (46% and 22%, respectively), workplace ministries (28% and 18%, respectively) or church planting (25% and 12%, respectively).

The age of a church leader has some connection to the types of activities his or her church engages in. Here, church leaders younger than 45 years old demonstrate more of an evangelistic emphasis. In this case, they report greater involvement in outreach events (75%, compared to 63% of older church leaders), church planting (23%, compared to 16% of older church leaders) or short-term mission trips (41%, compared to 31% of older church leaders)—all projects that mesh well with young pastors' reported interest in producing conversions. Elsewhere, church leaders over and under age 45 track closely in their engagement decisions, though older leaders stand out in higher reports of charity fundraising (74%, compared to 63% of younger church leaders).

THE GLOBAL REACH OF THE UK CHURCH

When it comes to the parameters of the UK Church's social justice and mission work, two-thirds of active Christians (65%) believe global and local efforts should be given equal attention. This conviction deepens among older Christians (70% of those over age 45). Knowing that older UK adults have greater representation among active Christians, this means churches are likely made up of individuals hoping for opportunities to reach people within their own neighbourhoods and around the world. This approach might already seem clear, but it stands in contrast to church leaders' (53%) and younger active Christians' (40%) common opinion that local work takes precedence. A number of Barna studies indicate a trend of younger Christians favouring local initiatives, possibly because growing up in a virtual, digital world makes tangible, personal efforts feel even more impactful.

WHAT'S THE IDEAL BALANCE BETWEEN GLOBAL AND LOCAL MISSION?

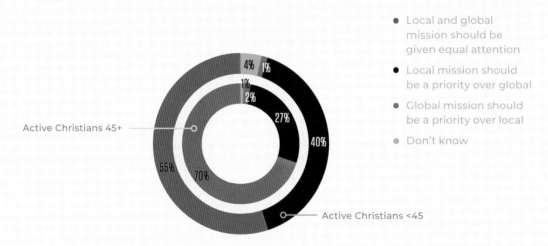

- Local and global mission should be given equal attention
- Local mission should be a priority over global
- Global mission should be a priority over local
- Don't know

Active Christians 45+

Active Christians <45

4% 1%
1%
2%
27%
40%
55%
70%

April 2017, n≈1,170 active UK Christians.

Beyond the UK, churches are most involved in Europe (63%) and Sub-Saharan Africa (53%), according to church leaders. More than a third (35%) contributes to work in the Middle East and North Africa. Church leaders, however, believe it is more important to support a specific cause than to support a specific region (23% 'strongly' + 44% 'somewhat' agree).

WHERE UK CHURCHES FOCUS ON SUPPORTING MISSION

According to church leaders

3%
North America

63%
Europe

35%
Middle East
& North Africa

15%
Latin America
& the Caribbean

53%
Sub-Saharan Africa

19%
South Asia

8%
Russia
& Central Asia

15%
East Asia

14%
Southeast Asia

5%
South Pacific

April–May 2017, n=302 UK church leaders.

A VISION FOR SOCIAL JUSTICE

When it comes to issues that could generally be categorised as social justice concerns, the UK Church's leaders and members mostly agree on what they want to support, as congregations or as individuals. In the local church, many Christians should expect to find some like-minded leadership and chances to channel their altruism into relevant programmes and campaigns.

Active Christians are most interested in giving or volunteering to alleviate forms of poverty (53% global, 50% local). There are some notable age differences when looking at the relatively political concerns that active Christians see as important to support. For example, those under age 45 are more likely than their elders to select the refugee crisis (29% vs. 22% of active Christians age 65+) or racial reconciliation (12% vs. 6% of active Christians age 65+), while the oldest age grouping ranks religious freedom higher (33% of active Christians age 65+ vs. 20% of active Christians under age 45).

Church leaders especially feel their churches should help the poor locally (60%), though they lag behind churchgoers in emphasis on international needs like global poverty assistance (40% vs. 53%) or child rights (10% vs. 19%). Other Barna studies have also shown church leaders are most rooted in their own region—not an unexpected tendency, considering that their influence is often required or sought out in local needs, which may present themselves more frequently and immediately than global ones. But that doesn't mean other broader concerns aren't on their radar: While church leaders likely want to prove effective locally where they are planted, they agree with active Christians that it's important to do what they can to help vulnerable

HOW SHOULD THE UK CHURCH SUPPORT SOCIAL JUSTICE?

When it comes to financial donations or volunteering for a cause, which three of the following social issues do you consider to be most important for you / your church to support?

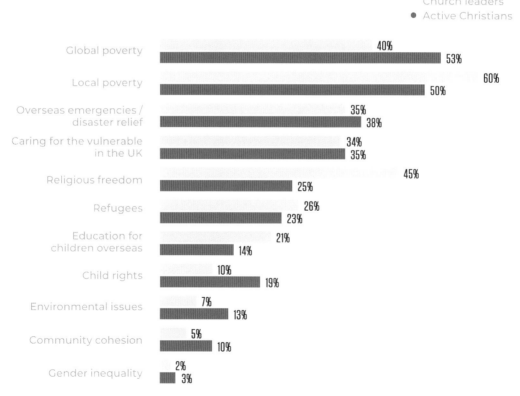

Church leaders
● Active Christians

	Church leaders	Active Christians
Global poverty	40%	53%
Local poverty	60%	50%
Overseas emergencies / disaster relief	35%	38%
Caring for the vulnerable in the UK	34%	35%
Religious freedom	45%	25%
Refugees	26%	23%
Education for children overseas	21%	14%
Child rights	10%	19%
Environmental issues	7%	13%
Community cohesion	5%	10%
Gender inequality	2%	3%

April 2017, *n*=1,170 active UK Christians; April - May 2017, *n*=302 UK church leaders.

Surveys for active Christians and church leaders used slightly different language for some causes; here, 'child rights' was also described as 'human rights', and 'community cohesion' was also described as 'racial reconciliation'.

populations (35% active Christians, 34% church leaders), victims of international disasters (38% active Christians, 35% church leaders) and refugees (23% active Christians, 26% church leaders).

Likely because of professional ties and implications, church leaders have a vested interest in contributing funds and time to support religious freedom or the persecuted Church (45%), which is much less of a priority among active Christians (25%).

UK CHURCHES' INVESTMENT IN SOCIAL JUSTICE

How involved would you say your church is in each of the following social issues?

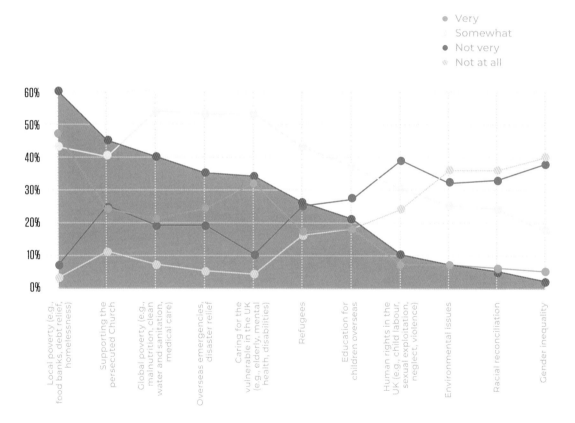

April–May 2017, n=302 UK church leaders.

Barna also asked church leaders to describe their church's actual level of involvement in each of these social justice causes, and, again, they seem to be making good on good intentions. Specifically, church leaders prove their local focus in saying their churches are deeply involved in helping the UK's poor (47% 'very') or vulnerable (32% 'very').

Some of the gaps between priority and activity could outline social justice projects and campaigns for which churches might consider a charity partnership—relationships we'll observe at length in the following chapter.

SUPPLY & DEMAND

COMPARING THE UK CHURCH'S CONTRIBUTIONS AND THE GENERAL PUBLIC'S EXPECTATIONS

● Needs that UK adults want churches to address*
● Needs that churches report addressing**

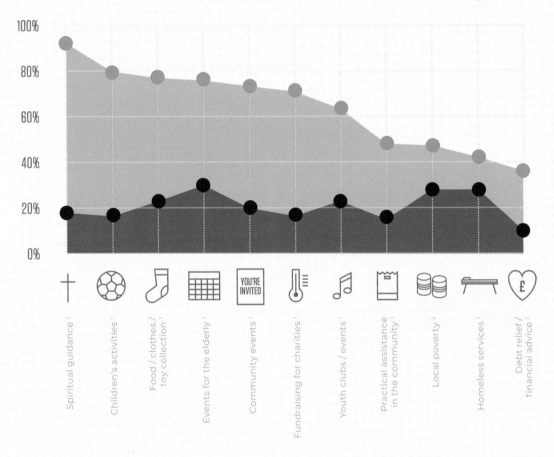

*Based on UK adults' answers to the following two questions:
- [1] What, if anything, does your community need that you feel Christian churches could provide?
- [2] If a Christian church organised an activity or campaign on any of the following issues, which, if any, would you be willing to support?

**Based on UK church leaders' answers to the following two questions:
- [1] Now, thinking about the specific ways your church engages with mission, both local and global, which of the following does your church engage in?
- [2] How involved would you say your church is in each of the following social issues? (% who say their church is 'very' involved)

There are a handful of global and local causes in which the UK public may welcome—or even collaborate with—the Church's work. How do these align with the activities and campaigns UK church leaders say they embrace? For the most part, congregations' level and variety of engagement is exceeding expectations. However, when it comes to some of the pressing or political matters of the day, there appear to be gaps in Christian leadership.

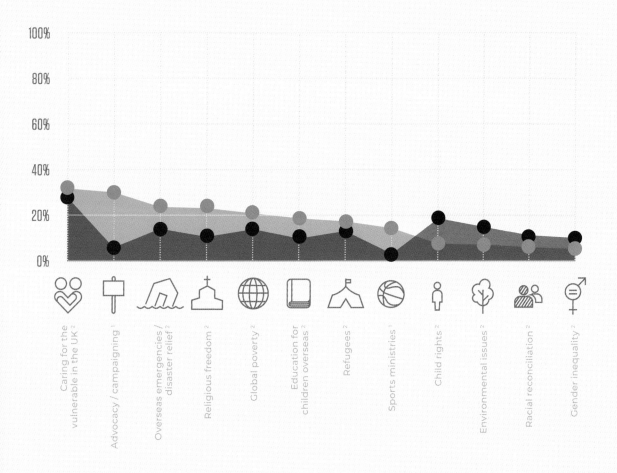

April 2017, n=2,054 British adults; April–May 2017, n=302 UK church leaders.

Surveys for all adults and church leaders used slightly different language for some causes: here, 'children's activities' was also described as 'children's ministry', 'spiritual guidance' was also described as 'pastoral care', 'racial reconciliation' was also described as 'community cohesion', 'religious freedom' was also described as 'supporting the persecuted church' and 'child rights' was also described as 'human rights'.

AT A GLANCE

SIX IN 10 CHURCH LEADERS (60%) FEEL THAT APPROACHING SOCIAL JUSTICE AND EVANGELISM IN TANDEM WILL BE THE WAY FORWARD.
Most church leaders believe mission work will also be increasingly effective in the future.

UK CHURCH LEADERS LOOK FIRST TO GOVERNMENTS, CHARITIES OR LAYPEOPLE TO ADDRESS MOST SOCIAL JUSTICE CONCERNS.
With the exception of local volunteering, UK church leaders rarely place primary responsibility for justice needs on those in the Church.

NEARLY THREE-QUARTERS OF CHURCH LEADERS (72%) SAY THEIR CHURCH HAS A CLEARLY DEFINED STRATEGY FOR MISSION.
At the core of these strategies is financial partnership with Christian organisations that are respected in their sector.

ACTIVE CHRISTIANS ARE EAGER TO SUPPORT SOCIAL JUSTICE AND MISSION BY GIVING TO THEIR CHURCH *AND* CHARITIES.
UK adults in general, and non-Christians especially, are more hesitant to get involved with campaigns run by a Christian church.

PARTNERS FOR THE FUTURE

4

Whose job is social justice?

It's a big question—one that church leaders in the UK wrestle to answer. And, at this time, they don't plan on the Church playing an outsize role in attending to society's ills and injustices. But this report reveals they are open to partnering with capable charities and responding to the prodding of their empathetic churchgoers, so it's possible the job description of the Church in the UK may continue to shift.

TAKING TURNS: WHO IS RESPONSIBLE FOR WHAT?

Barna's survey presented UK church leaders with broad categories of local and global need and then asked them: Who is responsible for addressing each?

Church leaders designate community volunteering and support (49% local, 57% global) and advocacy work (36% local, 40% global) as tasks that should be shared equally by *all* individuals. They look first to the government when it comes to relief for large-scale problems like poverty (50% local, 59% global) or natural disasters (58% local, 66% global).

Church leaders hope members of the Church play at least some part in many social justice causes, especially in the UK. Almost half (47%) prefer that Christians take the lead in local volunteering, and about one in four says they are accountable for advocacy work (27%) and helping the poor (23%) in their own region. Globally, they also think Christians should be some of the crucial players in community support (41%) and policy changes (21%). These UK perspectives are similar to those of church leaders in the U.S.: In a study commissioned by Compassion International, Barna found that, while American pastors see international poverty primarily as a government responsibility (30%), they still want the Church to lead in caring for the poor globally (26%) and especially locally (34%).[4]

Church leaders place only a moderate burden on charities, usually for causes like political advocacy (23% local, 20% global), poverty alleviation (23% local, 19% global) and disaster relief (22% local, 28% global). This is true even of specifically Christian charities. Church leaders seem to welcome but not necessarily depend on the leadership of faith-based organisations in advocacy (26% local, 27% global), global disaster relief (21%) and helping the poor (18% local, 20% global).

While church leaders primarily task the government or individuals for any needs of the public, they do want to have a presence in political advocacy (35% local, 27% global) and embrace an obligation in community support (33% local, 26% global). These responses may reflect church leaders' impression, mentioned earlier, that their ultimate missional objective is to equip the individual Christians in their congregation.

Of course, all of this pertains to how UK church leaders *prefer* the various societal duties be distributed. After asking church leaders who they see as most responsible for certain issues, Barna then asked them to identify who actually does the most to address them. Their responses suggest they perceive some discrepancies between who *should* and who *does* care for needs in the UK and beyond.

For instance, across the board, church leaders assume both secular and

Christian charities are doing a greater proportion of the work than they should have to. Meanwhile, there are a few areas where they leave room for politicians and individual citizens to step up. Church leaders think those in their own field are meeting expectations, though they may want clergy to be even *more* active and influential in political advocacy. As mentioned earlier in this report, the general public is more prone to see the Church as over-involved in politics, so this may be a tension that church leaders will have to be mindful of as they determine when and how to use their voice on politically charged issues.

To church leaders, poverty presents one of the greatest leadership gaps. Many recognise charities (50% local, 58% global), including Christian ones (39% local, 47% global), working hard in the trenches of poverty alleviation. As mentioned earlier, however, a majority of church leaders thinks governments should bear primary responsibility in this area. It's likely that church leaders still welcome this effort from charities, but simply want political powers to assist further.

There is another explicitly spiritual task in which, notably, church leaders are unlikely to invite the involvement of Christian charities: local evangelism. Sharing the gospel in the UK is something they feel is best left to individual Christians (72%) and church leaders (68%), rather than faith-based organisations (6%).

CALLING IN REINFORCEMENTS: OPINIONS OF CHARITY PARTNERS

Public trust in charities isn't necessarily a guarantee and has been particularly fraught in recent years.[5] But many UK church leaders identify these groups as valuable allies. For the most part, church leaders would rather partner with an established charity than attempt to start their own independent mission programme (79%). This is especially true of smaller churches, whose eagerness likely stems from a greater need for the capacity and resources that charities can provide. The majority of church leaders (54% 'strongly' + 34% 'somewhat') prefers to work alongside charities with a Christian identity rather than with secular aid organisations, though they are open to looking beyond their own denomination.

Finding individual mission partners to support seems to be a more

Church leaders assume both secular and Christian charities are doing a greater proportion of the work than they should have to

HOW UK CHURCH LEADERS DELEGATE SOCIAL JUSTICE

- Local needs
- Global needs

Which group should be most responsible for ...? *Select up to two parties for each.*

	All individuals		Christians		Church leaders		Christian charities		Charities		The government	
Disaster relief	40%	40%	16%	9%	16%	7%	11%	21%	22%	28%	58%	66%
Community support	49%	57%	47%	41%	33%	26%	14%	14%	12%	8%	9%	14%
Poverty	35%	45%	23%	16%	17%	10%	18%	20%	23%	19%	50%	59%
Advocating for political change	36%	40%	27%	21%	35%	27%	26%	27%	23%	20%	18%	28%

Which group is actually doing the most for ...? *Select up to two parties for each.*

	All individuals		Christians		Church leaders		Christian charities		Charities		The government	
Disaster relief	20%	10%	11%	12%	10%	4%	20%	39%	47%	55%	49%	40%
Community support	36%	35%	48%	39%	29%	24%	14%	24%	27%	30%	5%	7%
Poverty	13%	10%	20%	16%	15%	7%	39%	47%	50%	58%	23%	24%
Advocating for political change	21%	13%	17%	12%	24%	21%	34%	47%	48%	52%	12%	15%

April–May 2017, *n*=302 UK church leaders.

relational, local decision for churches; half of leaders (49%) agree at least somewhat that these connections should come from within their church, rather than a mission organisation.

PASTORS' FIRST CHOICES FOR CHARITY PARTNERSHIPS

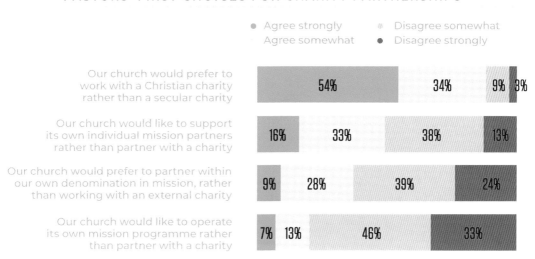

● Agree strongly　　⌗ Disagree somewhat
Agree somewhat　　● Disagree strongly

Our church would prefer to work with a Christian charity rather than a secular charity
54% | 34% | 9% | 3%

Our church would like to support its own individual mission partners rather than partner with a charity
16% | 33% | 38% | 13%

Our church would prefer to partner within our own denomination in mission, rather than working with an external charity
9% | 28% | 39% | 24%

Our church would like to operate its own mission programme rather than partner with a charity
7% | 13% | 46% | 33%

April–May 2017, n=302 UK church leaders.

Though church leaders want organisational partners that share their religious beliefs, they support Christian charities that partner with non-Christian organisations (73% 'definitely' + 'probably') or work in the secular sector (92% 'definitely' + 'probably'). This may be something that church leaders look for when choosing partners in social justice and mission work: a capable charity that they trust to uphold their Christian values and to maintain credible, strategic connections in the field-at-large.

Nearly all churches (92%) do in fact support a Christian charity already, and church leaders believe the rest of their faith community—whether other churches (88%), individual Christians (78%) or denominations (65%)—should also consider affiliating with faith-based organisations.

Church leaders support Christian charities that work with non-Christian organisations or in the secular sector

IS IT APPROPRIATE FOR A CHRISTIAN CHARITY TO WORK IN THE SECULAR SECTOR?

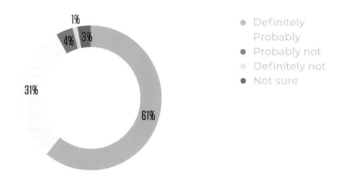

1%
4% 3%
31%
61%

- Definitely
- Probably
- Probably not
- Definitely not
- Not sure

IS IT APPROPRIATE FOR A CHRISTIAN CHARITY TO WORK WITH A NON-CHRISTIAN CHARITY?

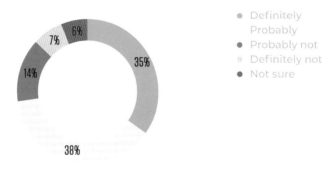

6%
7%
14%
35%
38%

- Definitely
- Probably
- Probably not
- Definitely not
- Not sure

April - May 2017, n=302 UK church leaders.

THE CONNECTIONS THAT DRIVE MISSION

A Q&A WITH DR. KRISH KANDIAH

Q How can we help the UK Church stand with some of the world's most vulnerable communities (the homeless, elderly, children, refugees, etc.) and demonstrate together the difference that faith is making?

Firstly, and most importantly, the priorities of scripture should set the priorities for our church's life and mission. The Bible is consistently clear about God's special attention to the poor and vulnerable, especially the widow, the orphan and the stranger. If we pay attention to that, it has to inspire the Church to prioritise sacrificial service on behalf of the world's most vulnerable.

Secondly, many of us are not naturally exposed to the Church globally. Our churches can be the places that inform and educate Christians about what is happening around the world, as well as inspiring them to pray and take action.

Thirdly, most of us have very little connection to the global Church or helping those living in poverty in our daily lives, work and activities. It is all too easy to set up a standing order, attend a prayer meeting and feel our part is played. But there are ways that the Church

DR. KRISH KANDIAH

Activist, author and theologian

Dr. Kandiah is the founding director of Home for Good, a charity seeking to find loving homes for children in the care system. His latest book, *God Is Stranger*, examines radical hospitality as a route to intimacy with God.

can provide catalytic connections so that the average Christian can form genuine, mutually beneficial relationships with those who are suffering—both in our communities and around the world. I'd love to see more church-to-church partnerships where we in the West are receivers as well as givers of wisdom, insight, people and prayer.

Q How can churches develop meaningful, innovative connections with relevant social justice agendas?

We live in a hyper-connected world where it is easier than ever to just travel between continents, but also, thanks to digital innovation, we have instantaneous communication with anyone on the planet who has an internet connection. Sadly, this has not yet had a revolutionary affect on the way that many Christians think about mission. Most Christians still have the misperception that mission is something we in the West do to the rest of the planet. But because it is easier than ever to get live information as to what our sisters and brothers are facing, it is also easier than ever for us to learn from Christians who are facing extreme poverty. This attitude can help to facilitate meaningful, innovative connections between churches and relevant social justice agendas.

Q How can leaders in the UK learn from global faith and community development work to help churches in the UK effect change more successfully?

Better communication between Christians in the UK and the wider world will help us to be rid of any unconscious superiority complex and develop a posture of humility in relating to our brothers and sisters. It is not right to assume we have all the answers and resources and our international Church family has all the problems. Spending time with Christians from other contexts quickly dispels that myth. It teaches us the power of hospitality, that programmes are not always the answer and

> 'It is not right to assume we have all the answers and resources and our international Church family has all the problems'

that some of our traditional well-meaning responses can make things worse rather than better. We need to go the extra mile to understand and listen to leaders in parts of the world where Western Christians have sought to help with aid and development to make sure that how we are helping is appropriate and genuinely helpful.

Q How can church leaders and Christians navigate politicised tension as they fulfil a calling to enact justice and meet needs? What would you recommend to leaders who struggle

The disparity often comes because of the kind of political issues Christians choose to speak out about. When Christians spend most of their time angrily defending their own rights or trying to impose our moral framework on a resistant culture, we are labelled as too political and we do not serve well the reputation of Jesus. When Christians can be seen speaking up for the marginalised and dispossessed, we rarely get dismissed so easily. For example, the Church's engagement with the Grenfell Tower victims or the championing of the needs of Muslim refugees from Syria were welcomed examples of the Church obeying scripture's imperative to 'Speak up for those who cannot speak for themselves, for the rights of all who are destitute. Speak up and judge fairly; defend the rights of the poor and needy' (Proverbs 31:8-9, NIV). I believe it is time to speak out on different issues: advocating for those with Down's Syndrome, dementia or mental health issues; forwarding the debates on identity; alleviating root causes of poverty and lifting people out of poverty; putting ourselves forward for adoption and fostering children in the care system; or welcoming refugees and those who are marginalised in our communities.

GLOBAL STRATEGIES

Nearly three-quarters of church leaders (72%) say their church has a clearly defined strategy for supporting mission. What do they see as their steps forward?

When active Christians and church leaders are asked to identify the three primary ways they think their churches should engage, the top response is yet another endorsement of charity partners: financial support of organisations working in mission and social justice (79% and 75%, respectively). Majorities (66% and 53%, respectively) also mention educating the congregation on issues relating to global mission as a starting point.

For some activities, active Christians are more keen than their leaders to get involved. For instance, regular prayer for global mission is a high priority for active Christians, but much less so for church leaders (61% and 44%, respectively). Interestingly, half of church leaders who say their church is 'very' effective in mission (50%) list prayer as one of the top ways they participate in global mission. Overall, church leaders should take note that their congregants want to engage in corporate prayer for the world's needs and injustices, and this spiritual contribution could also be a catalysing activity.

Active Christians also place greater emphasis on approaching global mission through advocacy (45%, compared to 26% of church leaders). This particular activity, often framed within social justice work, may feel like a public conflict for church leaders. As this study also shows, few UK adults, especially non-Christians, see political advocacy as a task for the Church to undertake, and there is rarely easy agreement on the best policies that could improve society. Regardless of whether churches should get involved in a more formal way in advocacy, active Christians may be inclined to take it upon themselves: After all, they are more likely than church leaders to say they want members to be encouraged to do global mission activities on their own (38%, compared to 21% of church leaders).

Sending members to serve abroad for short periods of time is lower on the list of priorities for both active Christians and church leaders, and those who do want to organise these ventures prefer that it be handled internally, without the external help of a Christian charity. As this study has mentioned repeatedly, the larger the church, the more engaged they are likely to be in this kind of costly endeavour: Church leaders of congregations with 100 or more people are twice as likely to include mission trips in their strategy (28%, compared to 10% of smaller churches).

> Congregants want to engage in corporate prayer for the world's needs and injustices

Church leaders: How does your church prioritise different ways of doing global mission?
● Active Christians: What activities should your church prioritise when doing global mission?

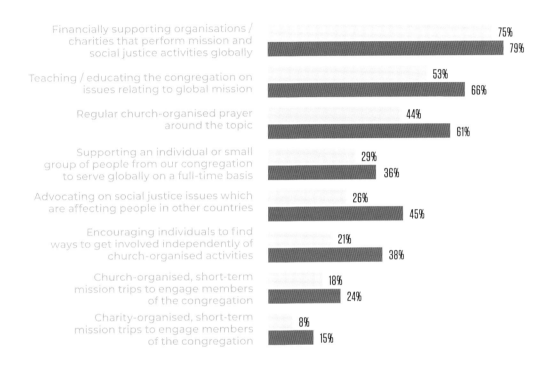

Financially supporting organisations /
charities that perform mission and
social justice activities globally — 75% / 79%

Teaching / educating the congregation on
issues relating to global mission — 53% / 66%

Regular church-organised prayer
around the topic — 44% / 61%

Supporting an individual or small
group of people from our congregation
to serve globally on a full-time basis — 29% / 36%

Advocating on social justice issues which
are affecting people in other countries — 26% / 45%

Encouraging individuals to find
ways to get involved independently of
church-organised activities — 21% / 38%

Church-organised, short-term
mission trips to engage members
of the congregation — 18% / 24%

Charity-organised, short-term
mission trips to engage members
of the congregation — 8% / 15%

April 2017, n = 1,170 active UK Christians, 302 UK church leaders.

HOW UK CHRISTIANS GIVE

Though UK church leaders are clearly amenable to charity partners and rely on them in strategies for global justice and mission, they are also protective of their church funding. A solid majority of UK church leaders (69%) believes that every member should give at least some amount of money to the church, and they have a firm conviction that this generosity cannot be treated as interchangeable with other faith-based charity donations. Three in five church leaders (61%) feel (including 35 percent 'strongly' so) that it would be unacceptable for a church member to give to a Christian charity instead of their own church. Leaders of churches who work with charities are likely not opposed to churchgoers' interest in supporting the organisation, but wish for it to not detract from the potential of their church's partnership (or from their weekly offering in general).

These church leaders need not worry, as the survey shows that very few active Christians give either only to their church (3%) or only to charities (2%). Instead, active Christians usually either favour the Church with their giving or give equally to both church and Christian organisations. This reflects a theme in other Barna studies: Compassionate and generous individuals rarely limit their focus to one area or cause. Instead, the more they care, the more they care.

Overall, nine of 10 active Christians (90%) indicate that they make some financial offering to their church, even when they also donate to charities. About one in five (22%) distributes their giving equally, while roughly half contribute to their church primarily (48%).

Younger active Christians are actually even more likely to direct their generosity toward the Church; half of those under age 45 (52%) give mostly to their church and some to charity. Many older active Christians strike this

Roughly half of active Christians give primarily to their church and some to Christian charities

DISTRIBUTING DONATIONS

I primarily give to my church and give some to Christian charities

I prefer to only give to my church

I give to both my church and Christian charities equally

I primarily give to Christian charities and also allocate some of my giving to my church

I prefer to only give to Christian charities

None of these

April 2017, n=1,170 active UK Christians

particular balance (46%), but they are also more likely to split their donations equally between their local church and Christian causes (25% of those over 45, compared to 13% of younger Christians).

According to church leaders, the main opportunity for Christians to donate money or goods through their church is the weekly offering (89%). Other common options include collections for food or clothing banks (86%), the church's specific activities or ministries (79%), global (78%) or local (56%) natural disasters, as well as global (71%) or local (61%) mission organisations.

Another popular avenue of Christian giving is child sponsorship. Half of active Christians have sponsored a child through a charity, either presently (25%) or at some point in the past (26%). Even if they don't participate, most active Christians (99%) are familiar with this model of helping children in need.

OPPORTUNITIES FOR CHURCH MEMBERS TO DONATE GOODS AND / OR MONEY

Weekly offering collection	89%
Food / clothes bank collection	86%
Collection for your church's activities or ministries	79%
Collection for crises or natural disasters globally	78%
Collection for a global mission organisation	71%
Collection for a local missions organisation	61%
Collection for crises or natural disasters locally	56%
Other organised giving / collections	49%
Collection for church members who have financial needs	37%

April–May 2017. n=302 UK church leaders.

GENEROSITY: FROM THE PULPIT

Church leaders believe the most important reason that Christians should be generous is to reflect God's own character, love (42%) and generosity (35%). A majority of them considers their own church to be generous (13% 'extremely' + 54% 'very'), and, accordingly, they make sure their congregants hear about the subject on a consistent basis.

Regular church attenders are being reminded at least occasionally of a Christian duty to give to and serve others. Nearly all church leaders (94%) say that they or another person gave a sermon within the last year on practising generosity with personal resources (e.g., time, money and goods). One in three (34%) says such a sermon was shared within the past month. Older church leaders are even more likely to provide teaching about giving; 35 percent of church leaders 45 and older, compared to one-quarter of younger church leaders (27%), say this has been covered in the past month.

A majority of church leaders also reports delivering sermons that include biblical perspectives of addressing poverty in the past six months (61%), if not more often (22% in the past month). The topic of poverty surfaces frequently in larger churches: In churches of 100 or more people, more than half of church leaders (55%) say someone has discussed poverty from the pulpit within the past three months. In smaller churches, 37 percent of church leaders report this frequency. It's possible that bigger congregations have more resources to give, more projects and programmes to discuss or more donors and volunteers to engage.

Beyond financial giving, churches encourage individual generosity through volunteering. Church leaders refer most to volunteer opportunities within the church's own ministries, such as youth group (88%) or in producing main services (88%), but they also direct volunteers toward community outreach activities (83%) or serving people in need (78%). Eighty-one percent of church leaders report that church members initiate volunteering opportunities themselves—an encouraging statistic revealing not only the drive of Christians, but also churches' awareness of the concerns of their congregations even beyond existing activities or ministries.

OPPORTUNITIES FOR CHURCHGOERS TO SERVE OTHERS OR VOLUNTEER

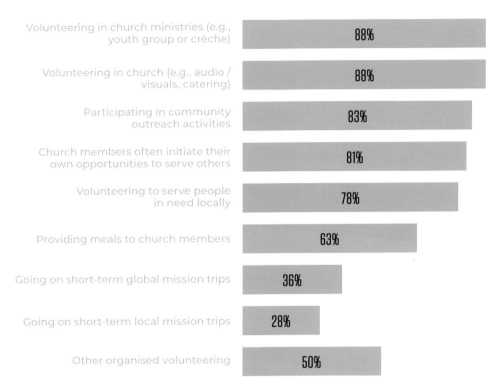

Volunteering in church ministries (e.g., youth group or crèche) — **88%**

Volunteering in church (e.g., audio / visuals, catering) — **88%**

Participating in community outreach activities — **83%**

Church members often initiate their own opportunities to serve others — **81%**

Volunteering to serve people in need locally — **78%**

Providing meals to church members — **63%**

Going on short-term global mission trips — **36%**

Going on short-term local mission trips — **28%**

Other organised volunteering — **50%**

April - May 2017, n=302 UK church leaders.

MAKING A CASE TO UNLIKELY ALLIES

In reviewing the data, it appears there's a promising line-up of church leaders, Christians and faith-based groups intent on working together to enact justice around the world, on behalf of the Church in the UK. But those outside of this group might require some extra convincing.

One in three UK adults (33%) says they would not get involved with *any* activity or campaign run by a Christian church—no matter the cause or social issue being addressed. Another one in five adults in the UK (20%) is simply unsure if they'd support a church-organised project. Among non-Christians, the percentage of those who are either opposed to or unclear on partnering with churches climbs to two-thirds (47% would not, 20% are unsure).

> One in three UK adults would not get involved with any activity or campaign run by a Christian church

LACK OF PUBLIC CONFIDENCE IN UK CHURCHES AS PARTNERS

If a Christian church organised an activity or campaign on any of the following issues, which, if any, would you be willing to support?

● All British adults
● Non-Christians

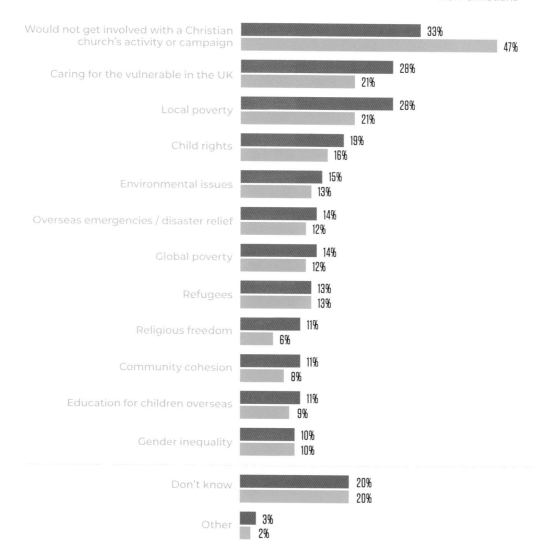

	All British adults	Non-Christians
Would not get involved with a Christian church's activity or campaign	33%	47%
Caring for the vulnerable in the UK	28%	21%
Local poverty	28%	21%
Child rights	19%	16%
Environmental issues	15%	13%
Overseas emergencies / disaster relief	14%	12%
Global poverty	14%	12%
Refugees	13%	13%
Religious freedom	11%	6%
Community cohesion	11%	8%
Education for children overseas	11%	9%
Gender inequality	10%	10%
Don't know	20%	20%
Other	3%	2%

April 2017, *n*=2,054 British adults.

The half of UK adults who are willing to support a cause alongside a church have vulnerable or poor populations at the front of their minds. Similar proportions say they would join in with a church to address local poverty through food banks, debt relief or combating homelessness (28%, including 21% of non-Christians) or to support the elderly, those with poor mental health or people with disabilities (28%, including 21% of non-Christians). One in five (19%) would help churches in championing child rights.

Presently, the outlook for multi-faith or interfaith initiatives in the increasingly secular context of the UK is bleak. Church leaders face a challenge to communicate the Church's calling and work to a sceptical public, especially the significant portion who have not yet made up their mind on whether they would associate with Christians' justice and mission work.

As the general population contemplates the Church's value to these causes, church leaders are still arriving at—and in some cases perhaps correcting—their own theories of how their churches should go out into the world. For example, looking at UK church leaders' descriptions of the

THEN AND NOW: UK CHURCH LEADERS PERCEIVE A SHIFT TOWARD SOCIAL JUSTICE

How has the relationship between evangelism and social justice, within the context of mission, changed over time?

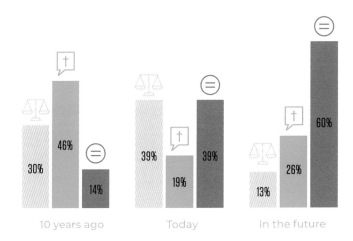

 More emphasis on social justice than evangelism

 More emphasis on evangelism than social justice

Equal importance for social justice and evangelism

April–May 2017. n=302 UK church leaders.

relationship between social justice and evangelism over time, church leaders sense there's been a significant shift toward justice in the past decade. Now, they anticipate a future in which social justice and evangelism are both crucial in accomplishing the Church's mission—an affirmation of active Christians' belief that, in mission, these aims should have equal importance.

The church leaders who embrace an equal emphasis on social justice and evangelism are optimistic about the future of mission

To UK church leaders, the forecast is favourable. They predict the Church's efforts will only improve; more than half (53%) say mission work will become more effective in the future. Additionally, the church leaders who embrace an equal emphasis on social justice and evangelism are even more optimistic that this particular approach is the right track (63%).

Even as the general population in the UK sorts through uncertain impressions of faith and its institutions, the Church shows signs of burgeoning confidence, benevolence and partnership. Perhaps in time the clarity of these Christians and their leaders will be catching.

A NEW CONVERSATION ABOUT SOCIAL JUSTICE AND MISSION

And why the UK Church's continued involvement
will depend on dialogue and collaboration

A significant faction of today's general population in the UK looks at the Church and wonders: 'What's the point?' A persuasive response might be to point to the many social justice and mission activities that churches are undertaking. In fact, the good that Christians do in the UK and around the world is well-documented, but apparently not well-understood. Why?

One reason may be that those *within* churches—leaders and attendees— seem to tell the story of the Church in different ways. Even within these specific groups, ideas about how to minister to and serve others are further diffused, often across generations. Though some broader beliefs may be shared (take heart: spiritual growth is still widely seen as essential to the Church's mission!), some of the discussions in or surrounding the Church's role in social action have broken down with time—or seem to be missing altogether.

As ministries consider how to better communicate and fulfil a call to social justice and mission, this study points to a few relationships that could use nurturing:

BETWEEN CHRISTIANS AND NON-CHRISTIANS

In spite of significant evidence—in this report and elsewhere—that the Church in the UK is generous and engaged in a range of needs, a sizeable percentage of the population is unsure or sceptical of its impact. And as rates of Christianity decline in the UK, so does the likelihood of meaningful and positive encounters with people of faith—like a recent headline from *The Guardian* pronounces, 'Christianity as default is gone'.[6] But these interfaith connections can be as powerful as they are rare. For instance, Barna's data shows public perceptions of *individual* Christians tend to be more favourable than perceptions of the UK Church at-large. Maybe, as the saying goes, it's hard to hate up-close. Individual churchgoers have organic opportunities to influence how others view the faith through direct, daily interactions that may elude church leaders or congregations as a whole. Active Christians who are committed to social justice and mission activities not only help improve the lives of others, but could help improve the reputation of the Church.

> Active Christians who are committed to social justice and mission activities not only help improve the lives of others, but could help improve the reputation of the Church

BETWEEN GENERATIONS

The proportion of Christians is decreasing not only generally, but by generation—meaning, the UK Church is an aging community, and young Christians and church leaders have fewer peers in the faith.

As a result, this study finds that some of the central differences across each sample seem to be correlated with generational divides. A UK adult's age might colour their opinion of Christian institutions—after all, one in five individuals between ages 18 and 34 doesn't even know how to describe the Church. A leader's age is linked with the strategies and activities that drive churches; for instance, many newer leaders exhibit a heightened urgency around evangelism, outreach and conversion. A churchgoer's age could inform their decisions to donate or get involved, as seen in older Christians' greater passion for disaster relief or religious freedom and younger Christians' greater empathy for political concerns like child rights or the refugee crisis.

Because of these and multiple other dissimilarities among age groups, UK church leaders need to embrace an intentionally multigenerational message. Are strategies for campaigns and partnerships cognisant of both older and younger church members' interests—where they align, as well as where they deviate? How does a church's local presence speak to the needs of emerging generations who lack positive paradigms of Christianity? How are younger churchgoers included and raised up to carry on the legacy of the Church—and can elders in the congregation be useful in that mentorship effort? Do programmes and departments promote intergenerational community by partnering people of different ages around common areas of passion, perhaps even ones that bridge other political or cultural divides?

BETWEEN CHURCH LEADERS AND THEIR CONGREGANTS

The active Christians in this study are just that: *highly* active and invested in their churches. Their responses offer an authentic glimpse of the people who are faithful to their faith community, and thus merit close consideration—especially because, at times, they differ profoundly from those of church leaders.

For example, active Christians indicate that they still see discipleship as a primary function of the Church—which is encouraging for church leaders, who typically see mission through the lens of discipleship, but may also worry their spiritual instruction is less relevant in an increasingly irreligious era. At the same time, active Christians are also *far* more likely than their leaders to prioritise aiding people in need, as well as supporting global poverty alleviation or participating in advocacy. The desire for this 'both / and' balance—to be both discipled for spiritual growth and equipped for social action—should guide church leaders discerning how to effectively use their voices and direct attention and resources. There's a good chance that those attending churches are less likely than those leading churches to draw stark lines between what constitutes 'social justice' or 'mission'.

BETWEEN THE CHURCH AND CHARITIES

Finally, let's look at the relationship between UK churches and charities. This partnership, which is already a familiar one, could help address the trust deficit facing both the Church and charities, if executed well. This symbiotic exchange helps churches be more effective in accomplishing their expressed social justice goals, while also bolstering organisations that, as church leaders

Joining forces with a
credible organisation
allows church
leaders to deepen
their involvement
in demonstrated
priorities, as well
as expand their
focus to issues
that may require
additional, on-the-
ground expertise

see it, do a greater share of the work than they should have to. Joining forces with a credible organisation allows church leaders to deepen their involvement in demonstrated priorities (like local poverty), as well as expand their focus to issues that may require additional, on-the-ground expertise (like overseas emergencies or refugee assistance). A large majority of UK church leaders sees value in partnering with a charity (usually, a Christian one respected in its sector).

Church leaders should anticipate that these alliances will be well-regarded by those within their churches as well: Active Christians are eager to give to a range of social justice causes and are enthusiastic about financially supporting both their churches *and* charities. Calling public attention to close collaboration with authorities in the field also couldn't hurt a church's credibility in the eyes of the general population, who need some convincing that backing church-led campaigns will be worth their while.

There might be many incentives and positive outcomes for the UK church that takes social justice seriously. But, ultimately, there is scriptural precedent for its engagement as well. As Dr. Paula Gooder mentions in her interview on page 21, the most important question to ask is, '*Why* do Christians do what they do'? Whatever a church's path forward, it should be paved in prayer—an activity that Christians consider to be crucial in participating in global mission.

The following pages and tables offer an extended look at some of the specific segments in which responses were consistently, and at times remarkably, different across the samples surveyed.

GENERAL UK POPULATION

Which of the following accurately describes your perception or opinion of the Christian Church? *Select all that apply.*

	Total	Age group	
	GENERAL UK POPULATION	UNDER AGE 45	AGE 45 OR OLDER
Good for the community	26%	18%	32%
Hypocritical (teaching one thing and doing another)	24%	24%	24%
Judgmental	23%	26%	20%
Not compatible with science	20%	21%	20%
Simplistic (does not have answers to the complicated questions of life)	17%	14%	19%
Focused on the needs of the community	14%	11%	17%
Collaborative with other Christian organisations	14%	11%	16%
Offers hope for the future	14%	11%	16%
Promotes social issues	13%	11%	14%

Continued: Which of the following accurately describes your perception or opinion of the Christian Church? *Select all that apply.*

	Total	Age group	
	GENERAL UK POPULATION	UNDER AGE 45	AGE 45 OR OLDER
Too involved in political issues	12%	11%	12%
Helps people meet their health or well-being needs	11%	9%	13%
Collaborative with other faiths	11%	8%	14%
Positive presence in local schools	11%	9%	12%
Relevant to my life	9%	7%	11%
Generous	7%	10%	6%
Internally focused	6%	6%	7%
Exclusive club	5%	5%	4%
Helps people meet their economic needs	5%	5%	4%
None of these	13%	14%	11%
Don't know	16%	19%	13%

Thinking about the churches in your area and any activities they do, read the following statements, then indicate whether or not you agree with it:

	Total	Age group	
	GENERAL UK POPULATION	UNDER AGE 45	AGE 45 OR OLDER
LOCAL CHRISTIAN CHURCHES ARE MAKING A POSITIVE DIFFERENCE IN YOUR COMMUNITY			
Strongly agree	6%	7%	6%
Tend to agree	29%	26%	30%
Tend to disagree	16%	18%	15%
Strongly disagree	10%	10%	10%
Don't know	39%	39%	39%
CHRISTIAN CHURCHES IN THE UK ARE MAKING A POSITIVE DIFFERENCE IN THE WORLD			
Strongly agree	7%	9%	5%
Tend to agree	26%	25%	27%
Tend to disagree	20%	18%	21%
Strongly disagree	11%	11%	11%
Don't know	36%	37%	35%

What, if anything, does your community need that you feel Christian churches could provide? *Select all that apply.*

	Total	Age group	
	GENERAL UK POPULATION	UNDER AGE 45	AGE 45 OR OLDER
Events for the elderly (e.g., befriending, meals)	30%	26%	34%
Homeless services (e.g., night shelters, soup kitchens, clothes)	28%	26%	29%
Shelter for the homeless	24%	22%	25%
Food / clothes / toy collection and distribution	23%	23%	22%
Youth clubs / events	23%	20%	25%
Church café / parents and toddlers / community events	20%	18%	23%
Activities for teens in the community	19%	17%	22%
Spiritual guidance	18%	16%	20%
Children's activities (e.g., holiday clubs, etc.)	17%	16%	17%
Fundraising for charities	17%	19%	15%
Practical assistance in the community (e.g., painting, gardening, etc.)	16%	14%	17%
Instilling / teaching morals or values	14%	11%	17%
Work in local schools	11%	11%	11%
Debt relief / financial advice	10%	10%	11%
Advocacy / campaigning	6%	8%	5%

Continued: What, if anything, does your community need that you feel Christian churches could provide? *Select all that apply.*

	Total	Age group	
	GENERAL UK POPULATION	UNDER AGE 45	AGE 45 OR OLDER
Sports ministries	3%	4%	2%
The church is already meeting the community needs	6%	4%	7%
None of these	10%	12%	8%
Don't know	31%	31%	31%

If a Christian church organised an activity or campaign on any of the following issues, which, if any, would you be willing to support? *Please select each campaign you would be willing to support.*

Note: See page 14 for non-Christians' answers.

	Total	Age group	
	GENERAL UK POPULATION	UNDER AGE 45	AGE 45 OR OLDER
Local poverty (e.g., food banks, debt relief, homelessness)	28%	27%	30%
Caring for the vulnerable in the UK (e.g., elderly, mental health, disabilities)	28%	25%	31%
Child rights (e.g., child labour, sexual exploitation, neglect, violence)	19%	22%	17%
Environmental issues	15%	16%	13%
Global poverty (e.g., malnutrition, clean water and sanitation, medical care)	14%	17%	12%
Overseas emergencies / disaster relief	14%	15%	13%
Refugees	13%	16%	11%
Community cohesion	11%	13%	10%
Education for children overseas	11%	14%	8%
Religious freedom	11%	11%	11%
Gender inequality	10%	15%	7%
Would not get involved with a Christian church activity or campaign	33%	29%	37%
Don't know	20%	25%	17%
Some other cause	3%	3%	2%

ACTIVE UK CHRISTIANS

Which of the following do you think should be top priorities at your church? *Please select top 3.*

	Total	Age group		Denomination					
	ACTIVE UK CHRISTIANS	UNDER AGE 45	AGE 45 OR OLDER	ANGLICAN	NON-ANGLICAN PROTESTANT	BAPTIST	METHODIST	CATHOLIC*	ALL PROTESTANT
Discipleship	58%	60%	57%	61%	57%	63%	51%	18%	59%
Worship	55%	39%	62%	59%	52%	42%	72%	86%	55%
Serving those in need	47%	51%	46%	51%	44%	43%	45%	60%	47%
Building community / relationships	43%	48%	40%	44%	42%	42%	48%	41%	43%
Evangelism	42%	45%	41%	34%	48%	53%	34%	40%	42%
Teaching / preaching	40%	41%	40%	37%	43%	51%	31%	37%	40%
Providing opportunities to serve in the church	4%	5%	3%	4%	3%	4%	3%	12%	4%
None of these	–	1%	–	–	1%	–	2%	–	–

*Sample size for Catholics is too small (*n* = 25) to be representative. Interpret with caution. The total sample, however, is representative of denominational distribution in the UK.

Which of the following best describes what you think mission looks like today?

	Total	Age group		Denomination					
	ACTIVE UK CHRISTIANS	UNDER AGE 45	AGE 45 OR OLDER	ANGLICAN	NON-ANGLICAN PROTESTANT	BAPTIST	METHODIST	CATHOLIC*	ALL PROTESTANT
Social justice and evangelism have equal importance	45%	35%	49%	44%	45%	52%	36%	52%	44%
Less focused on evangelism, more emphasis on social justice	38%	41%	37%	39%	38%	36%	52%	26%	39%
Less focused on social justice, more emphasis on evangelism	11%	14%	10%	10%	12%	7%	7%	8%	11%
Don't know	6%	10%	4%	6%	6%	5%	5%	13%	6%

Which of the following statements best describes the way you personally think local versus global mission should be prioritised?

	Total	Age group		Denomination					
	ACTIVE UK CHRISTIANS	UNDER AGE 45	AGE 45 OR OLDER	ANGLICAN	NON-ANGLICAN PROTESTANT	BAPTIST	METHODIST	CATHOLIC*	ALL PROTESTANT
Local mission should be a priority over global	31%	40%	27%	29%	33%	26%	35%	15%	31%
Local and global mission should be given equal attention	65%	55%	70%	68%	63%	68%	55%	78%	65%
Global mission should be a priority over local	2%	1%	2%	2%	2%	4%	2%	2%	2%
Don't know	2%	4%	1%	1%	3%	2%	7%	5%	2%

What activities should your church prioritise when doing global mission?
Please select your top 3 priorities.

	Total	Age group		Denomination					
	ACTIVE UK CHRISTIANS	UNDER AGE 45	AGE 45 OR OLDER	ANGLICAN	NON-ANGLICAN PROTESTANT	BAPTIST	METHODIST	CATHOLIC*	ALL PROTESTANT
Financially supporting organisations / charities that perform mission and social justice activities globally	79%	73%	81%	81%	77%	80%	88%	70%	79%
Teaching / educating the congregation on issues relating to global mission.	66%	58%	69%	68%	64%	68%	76%	66%	66%
Regular church-organised prayer around the topic	61%	62%	61%	62%	61%	72%	50%	39%	62%
Advocating on social justice issues which are affecting people in other countries	45%	49%	44%	46%	43%	48%	66%	51%	45%
Encouraging individuals to find ways to get involved independently of church-organised activities	38%	40%	36%	39%	37%	43%	34%	17%	38%
Supporting an individual or small group of people from our congregation to serve globally on a full-time basis	36%	43%	33%	31%	42%	56%	22%	2%	37%
Church-organised, short-term mission trips to engage members of the congregation	24%	28%	22%	18%	30%	25%	15%	9%	25%
Charity-organised, short-term mission trips to engage members of the congregation	15%	16%	14%	14%	16%	17%	8%	5%	15%

Continued: What activities should your church prioritise when doing global mission? *Please select your top 3 priorities.*

	Total	Age group		Denomination					
	ACTIVE UK CHRISTIANS	UNDER AGE 45	AGE 45 OR OLDER	ANGLICAN	NON-ANGLICAN PROTESTANT	BAPTIST	METHODIST	CATHOLIC*	ALL PROTESTANT
Other	2%	2%	2%	2%	2%	0%	1%	0%	2%
Our church shouldn't have a role in global mission	1%	1%	0%	1%	1%	0%	0%	0%	1%

What, if anything, does your community need that you feel Christian churches could provide? *Select all that apply.*

	Total	Age group		Denomination					
	ACTIVE UK CHRISTIANS	UNDER AGE 45	AGE 45 OR OLDER	ANGLICAN	NON-ANGLICAN PROTESTANT	BAPTIST	METHODIST	CATHOLIC*	ALL PROTESTANT
Events for the elderly (e.g., befriending, meals)	63%	64%	64%	65%	62%	66%	69%	59%	64%
Church café / parents and toddlers / community events	54%	51%	55%	54%	54%	60%	68%	28%	55%
Work in local schools	54%	54%	53%	57%	52%	53%	52%	24%	54%
Spiritual guidance	53%	56%	52%	52%	54%	54%	57%	55%	53%
Children's activities (e.g., holiday clubs, etc.)	51%	55%	49%	51%	52%	61%	60%	13%	52%
Activities for teens in the community	47%	55%	44%	45%	49%	56%	42%	57%	47%
Debt relief / financial advice	46%	52%	44%	44%	49%	52%	46%	21%	47%
Food / clothes / toy collection and distribution	45%	46%	46%	47%	45%	45%	53%	35%	46%
Youth clubs / events	44%	51%	42%	41%	48%	52%	47%	23%	45%
Practical assistance in the community (e.g., painting, gardening, etc.)	36%	42%	34%	33%	39%	41%	39%	28%	36%
Homeless services (e.g., night shelters, soup kitchens, clothes)	35%	36%	34%	35%	34%	32%	39%	54%	34%
Instilling / teaching morals or values	26%	26%	25%	23%	27%	32%	21%	37%	25%
Fundraising for charities	24%	23%	24%	26%	21%	17%	35%	40%	23%

Continued: What, if anything, does your community need that you feel Christian churches could provide? *Select all that apply.*

	Total	Age group		Denomination					
	ACTIVE UK CHRISTIANS	UNDER AGE 45	AGE 45 OR OLDER	ANGLICAN	NON-ANGLICAN PROTESTANT	BAPTIST	METHODIST	CATHOLIC*	ALL PROTESTANT
Advocacy / campaigning	23%	24%	22%	24%	22%	23%	27%	26%	22%
Shelter for the homeless	22%	27%	20%	22%	22%	20%	23%	18%	22%
Sports ministries	12%	21%	9%	10%	14%	11%	10%	4%	13%
The church is already meeting the community needs	14%	12%	15%	15%	13%	14%	12%	2%	14%
None of these	17%	56%	1%	14%	19%	19%	16%	23%	17%

When it comes to financial donations or volunteering for a cause, which three of the following social issues do you consider to be most important for you, personally, to support? *Select up to 3.*

	Total	Age group		Denomination					
	ACTIVE UK CHRISTIANS	UNDER AGE 45	AGE 45 OR OLDER	ANGLICAN	NON-ANGLICAN PROTESTANT	BAPTIST	METHODIST	CATHOLIC*	ALL PROTESTANT
Global poverty (e.g., malnutrition, clean water and sanitation, medical care)	53%	50%	54%	56%	51%	64%	57%	44%	53%
Local poverty (e.g., food banks, debt relief, homelessness)	50%	50%	51%	52%	49%	50%	44%	52%	50%
Overseas emergencies / disaster relief	38%	28%	42%	38%	37%	43%	46%	40%	38%
Caring for the vulnerable in the UK (e.g., elderly, mental health, disabilities)	35%	37%	34%	34%	35%	36%	44%	39%	35%
Religious freedom (e.g., the persecuted Church)	25%	20%	27%	20%	30%	39%	18%	4%	25%
Refugees	23%	29%	21%	24%	22%	23%	26%	44%	23%
Child rights (e.g., child labour, sexual exploitation, neglect, violence)	19%	30%	15%	17%	21%	19%	18%	25%	20%
Education for children overseas	14%	13%	14%	12%	15%	11%	10%	15%	13%
Community cohesion	10%	12%	9%	10%	10%	4%	8%	2%	10%
Gender inequality	3%	6%	2%	4%	3%	0%	0%	11%	3%
Environmental issues	13%	13%	14%	17%	10%	6%	19%	24%	13%
None of these	18%	56%	2%	15%	20%	19%	15%	23%	18%

UK CHURCH LEADERS

What is the denomination of your church?

	Total
Church of England (Anglican)	30%
Baptist	14%
Roman Catholic	10%
Independent (other)	9%
Other	8%
Church of Scotland / Presbyterian	7%
Independent (FIEC)	6%
Methodist	6%
Pentecostal (e.g., Elim, Assemblies of God)	5%
Church in Wales	2%
Lutheran	1%
NewFrontiers	1%
Apostolic	1%
United Reformed	1%
Congregational, Emerging / Fresh Expression, Orthodox, Salvation Army, Vineyard	0%

How effective do you think your church is at local mission as it is defined here?

[Local mission was defined as 'proclaiming the gospel and demonstrating the transformational love of Christ by caring for others and addressing their physical, social and spiritual needs, in your local community'.]

	Total	Age group		Church size	
	UK CHURCH LEADERS	UNDER AGE 45	AGE 45 OR OLDER	LESS THAN 100 ATTENDEES	100 OR MORE ATTENDEES
Very effective	12%	14%	11%	7%	18%
Somewhat effective	71%	77%	70%	72%	71%
Not very effective	15%	9%	17%	19%	10%
Not at all effective	2%	-	2%	3%	-

How would you describe the relationship between mission and social justice?

	Total	Age group		Church size	
	UK CHURCH LEADERS	UNDER AGE 45	AGE 45 OR OLDER	LESS THAN 100 ATTENDEES	100 OR MORE ATTENDEES
They are essentially the same	10%	11%	10%	8%	13%
They are different but integral to each other	76%	66%	79%	80%	72%
They are distinct from each other	13%	23%	10%	11%	14%
Not sure	1%	-	1%	1%	1%

Does your church have a clearly defined strategy for addressing or supporting mission?

	Total	Age group		Church size	
	UK CHURCH LEADERS	UNDER AGE 45	AGE 45 OR OLDER	LESS THAN 100 ATTENDEES	100 OR MORE ATTENDEES
Yes	72%	72%	71%	63%	82%
No	28%	28%	29%	37%	18%

How effective do you think your church is at global mission as it is defined here?

[Global mission was defined as 'proclaiming the gospel and demonstrating the transformational love of Christ by caring for others and addressing their physical, social and spiritual needs, internationally or outside your country'.]

	Total	Age group		Church size	
	UK CHURCH LEADERS	UNDER AGE 45	AGE 45 OR OLDER	LESS THAN 100 ATTENDEES	100 OR MORE ATTENDEES
Very effective	14%	11%	15%	8%	21%
Somewhat effective	51%	50%	51%	49%	53%
Not very effective	30%	34%	28%	34%	25%
Not at all effective	6%	5%	6%	10%	1%

Now thinking about the specific ways your church engages with mission, both local and global, which of the following does your church engage in? *Select all that apply.*

	Total	Age group		Church size	
	UK CHURCH LEADERS	UNDER AGE 45	AGE 45 OR OLDER	LESS THAN 100 ATTENDEES	100 OR MORE ATTENDEES
Pastoral care / visitation / counseling in community (e.g., bereavement, etc.)	92%	94%	92%	90%	96%
Children's ministry (e.g., holiday clubs, messy church, etc.)	79%	81%	79%	72%	89%
Food / clothes / toy collection and distribution	77%	72%	79%	72%	84%
Events for the elderly (e.g., befriending, meals)	76%	78%	76%	68%	86%
Work in local schools	76%	78%	76%	73%	81%
Church café / parents and toddlers / community events	73%	78%	71%	64%	83%
Fundraising for charities	71%	63%	74%	64%	80%
Prayer for social justice issues	67%	69%	66%	60%	75%
Evangelism / outreach events (e.g., with strong gospel message / call)	65%	75%	63%	59%	74%
Youth clubs / events	63%	66%	63%	51%	78%
Preaching on issues around social justice	63%	66%	62%	55%	74%
Worship focused around mission	57%	59%	56%	48%	68%
Practical assistance in the community (e.g., painting, gardening, etc.)	48%	50%	47%	37%	61%
Bible study around social justice issues	43%	44%	43%	35%	53%

Continued: Now thinking about the specific ways your church engages with mission, both local and global, which of the following does your church engage in? *Select all that apply.*

	Total	Age group		Church size	
	UK CHURCH LEADERS	UNDER AGE 45	AGE 45 OR OLDER	LESS THAN 100 ATTENDEES	100 OR MORE ATTENDEES
Homeless services (e.g., night shelters, soup kitchens, clothes)	42%	47%	41%	32%	55%
Debt relief / financial advice	36%	34%	37%	28%	46%
Short-term mission trips	33%	41%	31%	22%	46%
Advocacy / campaigning	30%	25%	32%	22%	39%
Workplace ministries	22%	19%	23%	18%	28%
Church planting	18%	23%	16%	12%	25%
Healing on the streets	16%	14%	16%	8%	24%
Sports ministries	14%	16%	14%	8%	22%

Thinking about how non-Christians view churches' mission activities, read the following statements, then indicate whether or not you agree with it:

	Total	Age group		Church size	
	UK CHURCH LEADERS	UNDER AGE 45	AGE 45 OR OLDER	LESS THAN 100 ATTENDEES	100 OR MORE ATTENDEES
NON-CHRISTIANS THINK YOUR CHURCH IS HAVING A POSITIVE IMPACT ON YOUR COMMUNITY					
Agree strongly	30%	36%	28%	22%	40%
Agree somewhat	56%	55%	57%	60%	52%
Disagree somewhat	13%	8%	14%	17%	7%
Disagree strongly	1%	2%	1%	1%	1%
NON-CHRISTIANS THINK THE CHURCH IS HAVING A POSITIVE IMPACT ON THE WORLD					
Agree strongly	5%	9%	4%	2%	8%
Agree somewhat	42%	47%	40%	37%	47%
Disagree somewhat	44%	34%	46%	48%	38%
Disagree strongly	10%	9%	10%	12%	7%

Compared to 10 years ago, do you think mission today has become more or less effective?

	Total	Age group		Church size	
	UK CHURCH LEADERS	UNDER AGE 45	AGE 45 OR OLDER	LESS THAN 100 ATTENDEES	100 OR MORE ATTENDEES
More effective	40%	39%	40%	42%	38%
Less effective	20%	19%	21%	23%	17%
No change in effectiveness	26%	19%	28%	21%	32%
Not sure	14%	23%	11%	15%	13%

Now thinking into the future, do you think mission will become more or less effective than it is today?

	Total	Age group		Church size	
	UK CHURCH LEADERS	UNDER AGE 45	AGE 45 OR OLDER	LESS THAN 100 ATTENDEES	100 OR MORE ATTENDEES
More effective	53%	55%	53%	53%	53%
Less effective	12%	11%	12%	13%	11%
No change in effectiveness	11%	2%	14%	8%	16%
Not sure	24%	32%	21%	26%	20%

Thinking about the way your church conducts global mission, read each of the following statements, then indicate whether or not you agree with it:

	Total	Church size	
	UK CHURCH LEADERS	LESS THAN 100 ATTENDEES	100 OR MORE ATTENDEES
SUPPORTING A SPECIFIC CAUSE IS MORE IMPORTANT THAN SUPPORTING A SPECIFIC REGION			
Agree strongly	23%	24%	22%
Agree somewhat	44%	43%	44%
Disagree somewhat	28%	27%	30%
Disagree strongly	5%	6%	4%
OUR CHURCH WOULD LIKE TO OPERATE ITS OWN MISSION PROGRAMME RATHER THAN PARTNER WITH A CHARITY			
Agree strongly	7%	7%	7%
Agree somewhat	13%	9%	8%
Disagree somewhat	46%	42%	51%
Disagree strongly	33%	41%	24%
OUR CHURCH WOULD LIKE TO SUPPORT ITS OWN INDIVIDUAL MISSION PARTNERS RATHER THAN PARTNER WITH A CHARITY			
Agree strongly	16%	17%	15%
Agree somewhat	33%	34%	33%
Disagree somewhat	38%	35%	40%
Disagree strongly	13%	15%	11%

Continued: Thinking about the way your church conducts global mission, read each of the following statements, then indicate whether or not you agree with it:

	Total	Church size	
	UK CHURCH LEADERS	LESS THAN 100 ATTENDEES	100 OR MORE ATTENDEES
OUR CHURCH WOULD PREFER TO WORK WITH A CHRISTIAN CHARITY RATHER THAN A SECULAR CHARITY			
Agree strongly	54%	59%	49%
Agree somewhat	34%	29%	39%
Disagree somewhat	9%	11%	7%
Disagree strongly	3%	1%	5%
OUR CHURCH WOULD PREFER TO PARTNER WITHIN OUR OWN DENOMINATION IN MISSION, RATHER THAN WORKING WITH AN EXTERNAL CHARITY			
Agree strongly	9%	11%	7%
Agree somewhat	28%	24%	32%
Disagree somewhat	39%	38%	40%
Disagree strongly	24%	27%	21%

1. Barna Group, *Talking Jesus: Perceptions of Jesus, Christians and Evangelism in England* (Ventura, CA: Barna Group, 2015), http://talkingjesus.org/2015-research/.

2. Sarah Eekhoff Zylstra, 'How Billy Graham Brokered World Peace Between Evangelism and Social Justice', *Christianity Today*, 23 February 2018, https://www.christianitytoday.com/news/2018/february/billy-graham-lausanne-wea-evangelism-social-justice.html.

3. Cinnamon Network, *Cinnamon Faith Action Audit*, 2016, http://www.cinnamonnetwork.co.uk/wp-content/uploads/2016/08/Cinnamon-Faith-Action-Audit-Report-2016.pdf.

4. Barna Group, *The Good News About Global Poverty* (Ventura, CA: Barna Group, 2018), 78.

5. nfpSynergy, 'Briefing: Everything Baroness Stowell needs to know about trust in charities', 25 April 2018, https://nfpsynergy.net/blog/briefing-everything-baroness-stowell-needs-know-about-trust-charities.

6. Harriet Sherwood, '"Christianity as default is gone": the rise of a non-Christian Europe', *The Guardian*, 20 March 2018, https://www.theguardian.com/world/2018/mar/21/christianity-non-christian-europe-young-people-survey-religion.

This study involved quantitative surveys with British adults, church leaders and active Christians.

Barna interviewed 302 church leaders for this study. An online survey was conducted from 6 April 2017 to 9 May 2017, and a phone survey was conducted from 28 April 2017 to 9 May 2017. Not all questions were included in the phone version of this survey in order to shorten the length of the live interview.

Barna also surveyed 2,054 British adults (18 and older, representative of the general population) and 1,170 active Christians (a panel recruited primarily from Christian media sources) in two separate shared polls online (both hosted by ComRes) from 6 April 2017 to 11 April 2017.

Barna is solely responsible for the analysis of the data.

GLOSSARY

- UK / British adult: A person over 18 who lives in the UK (this particular panel did not include those who live in Northern Ireland)
- Church leader: A UK adult who confirms that they currently lead a church or congregation in the UK
- Active Christian: A UK adult who actively engages in a minimum of monthly churchgoing, Bible reading and prayer
- Non-Christian: A UK adult who identifies with a religion other than Christian (selected Muslim, Hindu, Jewish, Sikh, Buddhist, other, none or declined to answer)

ACKNOWLEDGMENTS

D

First, Barna Global wishes to thank World Vision UK for their partnership on this study and the individuals on their team who made this project possible. Their organisation exemplifies the heart of social justice and mission by improving the lives of vulnerable children around the world, and we hope this study inspires the Church as much as their example.

We're grateful to our expert contributors—Roy Crowne, Paula Gooder and Krish Kandiah—for greatly enhancing this report with their insights.

The research for this study was coordinated by Brooke Hempell and Traci Hochmuth. Under the editorial direction of Roxanne Stone, Susan Mettes contributed written analysis and Alyce Youngblood completed and edited the report. Gareth Russell advised on the project vision and partnership. Doug Brown and Fiona Spence provided copy edits and proofreading. Annette Allen designed the cover, interior layout and data visualizations. Brenda Usery oversaw production. Jennifer Hamel coordinated as project manager.

Additional thanks for the support of our Barna colleagues: Amy Brands, Bill Denzel, Aly Hawkins, Pam Jacob, David Kinnaman, Steve McBeth, Caitlin Schuman, Jess Villa and Todd White.

BARNA GROUP is one of the leading research organisations focused on faith and culture. Barna's areas of expertise include religious trends in society, with an emphasis on Christianity, the faith of younger generations and the impact of digital trends on religion. Having conducted more than 1 million interviews since 1984, Barna has become a go-to source for insights for church leaders, businesses and non-profit organisations who want to determine their next right step.

BARNA GLOBAL was started in 2013, with a head office in London, to provide research-driven strategies with and for the Christian community in the UK and beyond.

People turn to Barna for its proven expertise in assessing faith trends as well as its compelling data-based journalism and data visualisation. Barna's studies are frequently cited in major media outlets such as *The Economist,* BBC, NPR, CNN, *USA Today,* the *Wall Street Journal,* Fox News, *Chicago Tribune,* Huffington Post, *The New York Times,* and the *Los Angeles Times.*

| www.barnaglobal.com | @BarnaGlobal

WORLD VISION focuses on three key areas: child protection, child health and emergency response. Since 1950, the organisation has been working to bring real hope to millions of children in the world's hardest places, as a sign of God's unconditional love. World Vision's local teams work in thousands of communities to bring about long-term change. With a worldwide presence, the organisation is quick to respond to emergencies like conflict and natural disasters and can use its influence and global reach to ensure that children are represented at every level of decision-making. If you would like to know more about how together we can serve the world's most vulnerable children, or to get in touch with World Vision UK, please contact churches@worldvision.org.uk.

| www.worldvision.org.uk

What Can Barna Do For You?

When you need to make a decision, you want good information to guide you. You want a trusted advisor who knows the times. For more than 30 years, Barna has been providing reliable data and actionable insights to the leaders of some of the most influential organisations of our day. Whatever decision you're trying to make, Barna can help.

Custom Research
Accurate, timely and affordable research for organisations, faith leaders, entrepreneurs and innovators

Barna Polls
Shared-cost research that provides strategic insights about pastors or general population at minimal cost

Consulting
Actionable recommendations for your organisation, grounded in research and an understanding of your context

Resources
Published research and insights for leaders and decision makers

Learn more at
barnaglobal.com
@BarnaGlobal

Discover
Listening to understand your unique needs and expectations

Design
Determining the best questions and methodology to produce meaningful and reliable findings

Gather
Ensuring that the data is accurate and representative of your key audiences

Analyse
Interpreting results and identifying key patterns, trends and insights

Deliver
Creating custom monographs, reports or presentations to fit your needs

Advise
Applying Barna's decades of knowledge and experience to give you confidence to take action

Stay Informed About Cultural Trends

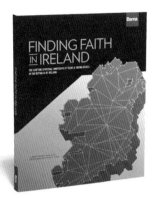

Finding Faith in Ireland
Go inside the minds of Irish youth as they wrestle with popular culture, societal expectations for success, and the nation's transforming spiritual identity.

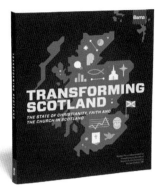

Transforming Scotland
A fascinating case study that provides actionable insights into how to do ministry and be the Church in a rapidly secularizing context.

Barna Trends 2018
A beautifully designed and engaging look at today's trending topics that includes new data, analysis, infographics, and interviews right at your fingertips.

Gen Z
Critical data to help the church effectively reach, serve and equip the emerging generation, helping them to confidently follow Jesus in today's rapidly changing culture.